Colorado

A History in Photographs

Colorado

A History in Photographs

by Dan Klinglesmith & Patrick Soran

Altitude Publishing Ltd.
Denver / Canmore / Vancouver

1998 © Altitude Publishing Ltd.

P.O. Box 309, 4255 South Buckley Road
Aurora, CO 80013

Cataloguing in Publication Data

ISBN: 1-55265-003-0
1. Colorado--History--Pictorial works. I.
Klinglesmith, Dan: 1955–; Soran, Patrick: 1953–
II. Title.
F777.K54 1998   978.8'03'0222
C98-910090-1

Altitude GreenTree Program

Altitude will plant twice as many trees as
were used in the manufacturing of
this product.

Design and Production Team

Concept	Stephen Hutchings
Art direction/design	Stephen Hutchings
Design/layout	Kelly Stauffer
Editor	Sabrina Grobler
Financial management	Laurie Smith

Printed in Canada by Friesen Printers

Note from the Publisher

Colorado's history has been richly docu-
mented by numerous photographers such
as William Henry Jackson. By and large, the
authors have utilized the collection of the
Colorado Historical Society (CHS), which
contains more than 500,000 images. More
than one book could easily have been
assembled from their archives.

The photographs chosen were selected
to represent Colorado from roughly the
mid-1800s to the 1950s. During this period,
black-and-white photography flourished as
a medium to record events. Seen in today's
light, it serves as an unadorned "magic
eye" through which to view the past. From
these grey-toned images we glimpse how
those who came before shaped the present
we experience today.

Stephen Hutchings

Stephen Hutchings
Publisher

Front Cover: Dick Charley,
a Ute farmer, posed for
this 1932 photo by E.J.
Floyd while Fox Newsreel
was filming Native
American dances near
Bayfield, Colorado.
Dick Charley; CHS.

Frontispiece: The hills sur-
rounding the former min-
ing camp of Aspen
boomed again in the late
1940s with the introduc-
tion of downhill skiing.
Colorado's world-renowned
"champagne powder"
would eventually make the
state synonymous with skiing at its finest.
*Skier at Aspen;
CHS F-537077*

Back Cover: This image of
the Garden of the Gods
has been attributed to photographer William Henry
Jackson. But, it was George
E. Mellen, one of Jackson's

studio employees, who
caught this evocative scene
of early visitors exploring
the stony monoliths of the
park north of
Colorado Springs.
*Garden of the Gods; CHS
3219D Portals of the
Gateway, Detroit Publishing.*

Table of Contents:
During Denver's heady
boom days of the late
1800s, dozens of railroads
tracked into the frontier
town. Tycoons Jay Gould
and Walter Cheesman con-
solidated the network,
erecting a central station
called Union Depot.
Nothing remains of this
original structure; today's
Beaux Arts facade dates
from 1914.
*Union Depot Welcome Arch;
CHS F-133862.*

Acknowledgements:
The authors would like to
acknowledge the fine con-
tributions of Rebecca Lintz,
Barbara Foley, Margi Aguiar
and Peg Ekstrand of the
Colorado Historical Society;
Jody McCabe of the Aspen
Historical Society, Marta
Sipeki of the Denver
Musuem of Natural History;
Deborah Dix of the Brown
Palace Hotel; Loreen Katz
of the Colorado Ski
Museum; Bruce Hanson of
the Denver Public Library,
Western History Collection;
Michelle Zupan of the Estes
Park Historical Museum;
Ester Mellott of the
National Mining Hall of
Fame and Museum; Dennis
Lesko of the Broadmoor
Hotel; Steve Shoe of Tourist
Railway Association
Incorporated; and Sue
Johnson-Einer of Mesa
Verde National Park.

Colorado
A History in Photographs

Table of Contents

Land of the Blue Sky People

*I*n the mid-1800s, no more than 4,000 Utes dwelled in Colorado's mountains. Only a few thousand nomadic Native Americans—Cheyenne, Arapaho, Pawnee, Lakota, Comanche and Kiowa—stalked great bison herds on the Eastern Plains. Colorado was the "Land of the Blue Sky People," a place where humans trod lightly on the grand terrain.

The 16th-century arrival of Spanish explorers and, more importantly their horses, had transformed Colorado's indigenous peoples' lifestyles. The Utes became masterful equestrians, as did the neighboring Plains Indians. Spanish ponies improved hunting and created decided advantages during inter-tribal skirmishes.

For the next 200 years, Colorado remained a virtual hinterland, a northern frontier to Spain's New Mexico colonial outposts. During the 17th and 18th centuries, global politics assigned Colorado to different nations. It appeared on various maps as part of New Spain, the Louisiana Territory of France, the Republic of Mexico and finally, the United States.

Gold discoveries in 1858 sounded a clarion call to thousands of Americans and immigrants seeking to get rich quick. It was also a death knell for Native Americans. Prospectors swarmed over the land, erecting temporary camps that would grow into towns. Conflicts inevitably arose. Within 10 years of the gold rush the Plains Indians succumbed to the U.S. Cavalry's might. Oklahoma reservations became their new home.

The Utes held onto their land longer. The Meeker Massacre of 1879, in which the Utes launched a murderous attack on the White River Indian Agency, marked the end to their traditional way of life. Full exile was the government's retaliation; many Utes were banished to Utah, while others took up residence in southern Colorado near the forgotten cities of the Ancestral Puebloans. Confined to small reservations amidst their once expansive domain, a permanent cloud now formed over the people who knew Colorado as the "Land of Blue Sky People."

Bottom: In 1820, Major Stephen Long lead an expedition into Colorado to explore the sources of the Platte, Arkansas and Red rivers. Included in his party of 19 men were a naturalist, a geologist, a map-maker, a landscape artist and topographers. They missed the headwaters of the great waterways, but added immensely to the scientific understanding of Colorado's Front Range.
Major Stephen Long; CHS #126.1.

Top: Photographer William Henry Jackson first explored the canyons of Mesa Verde in 1874, creating photographs that would shed light on the mysterious cliff dwellings of the Ancestral Puebloans. Jackson's later expeditions yielded other images such as this one of "Cliff Palace."
Mesa Verde Cliff Palace; CHS F-42628.

Top: Great herds of American bison, incorrectly termed buffalo, roamed the prairies and plateaus of Colorado. Generations of Native Americans relied on bison for food and materials for clothing, shelter and numerous bone tools. Sadly, by the late 1800s, Colorado's bison population was nearly decimated by Anglo-American hunters eager to supply railroad workers with meat and Eastern clothiers with shaggy hides.
Bison; CHS F 36279, Denver Museum of Natural History.

Bottom: During the late-1800's Hayden U.S. Geological Survey of the Territories, staff photographers such as William Henry Jackson recorded the rapidly disappearing culture of the Plain Indians with images such as this 1874 photo of a Lakota family outside their traditional home.
Teepee with Horse and Indians; CHS F-25787, Unident

Opposite: This late-1800's photo—Red Dog and an unidentified woman—depicts the distinctive attire of the Utes. Proficient traders, they bedecked themselves with goods acquired from New Mexico's Spanish markets as well as trading missions with Plains Indian tribes.
Red Dog and Woman; CHS F-33,533.

ZEBULON PIKE—THE LOST PATHFINDER

Lt. Zebulon Montgomery Pike and his 15 comrades were near present-day Las Animas, Colorado, when they spied something that "appeared like a small blue cloud" more than 100 miles away.

That "small blue cloud" turned out to be a 14,110-foot mountain west of present-day Colorado Springs which Pike called "Grand Peak." A later explorer, John Charles Frémont, was the one to name the peak after Pike by recording it on the maps he created.

Pike has been called the "Lost Pathfinder." The goal of his 1806 expedition was to trace the route of the Red River, the boundary line between the newly acquired Louisiana Purchase and existing Spanish territory. Pike miscalculated, however, and spent most of his days following the banks of the Arkansas River and then the Rio Grande River, believing them to be the Red River. Spanish soldiers finally corrected Pike when they took him and his party into custody near the Conejos River, deep within Spain's domain in the San Luis Valley.

Some historians hold to a different explanation for Pike's seemingly aimless wanderings. They maintain he was a secret agent on a reconnaissance expedition to Spanish-held lands. Pike's benefactor was General James Wilkinson, America's highest ranking general and recently appointed governor of the Louisiana territory. Along with traitorous Aaron Burr, Wilkinson nurtured a plan to create a "Southwestern Empire" which they would jointly rule. Direct knowledge of the land was crucial, and Pike was allegedly their eyes and ears.

Whatever the true reason for Pike's venture into the Rocky Mountains, his Spanish hosts proved to be hospitable and his poorly supplied band spent the rest of that winter in Santa Fe, New Mexico. Later, they were escorted to Chihuahua, Mexico and from there back to U.S. soil. Nearly two years after they started their journey, Pike and his men finally picked up the trail of the Red River near Natchitoches, Louisiana.

Photo: Zebulon Pike; CHS F-6835, WPA 2298.

ATTENTION!
INDIAN
FIGHTERS

Having been authorized by the Gov... raise a
Company of 100 day
U. S. VOL CAV
For immediate service against hostile Indians. I call u...
service to call at my office and enroll their names imme...
Pay and Rations the sa...
Volunteer Ca...
Parties furnishing their own horses will receive...
while in the service.
The Company will also be entitled to all horse...
Office first door East o...
Central City, Aug. 13, '...

Bottom: Frontiersman Kit Carson was described as being "rather below the medium height, with brown, curling hair, little or no beard, and a voice as soft and gentle as a woman's." Nonetheless, Carson figured prominently in Colorado history. He helped lead John C. Frémont's 1843 expedition into the central Rocky Mountains and later served as commander of Fort Garland, Colorado. In 1868, Carson and his family homesteaded near Boggsville, Colorado, but he and his wife died within a year, orphaning their children.
Kit Carson: CHS.

Top: This 1864 Central City poster called for soldiers to serve for 100 days in the Third Regiment of the Colorado Volunteer Cavalry. Their mission: rid the plains of hostile Indians. Tragically, they were successful, massacring more than 150 Cheyenne and Arapaho at Sand Creek in southeastern Colorado. *Indian Fighter Poster; CHS F-4232.*

partner Cerán St. Vrain, the adobe complex become the focal point of a trading empire along the Santa Fe Trail. Abandoned in 1852, the immense fort fell to its foundations but was faithfully reconstructed in 1976 from old drawings to depict what it was like during the 1840s. It is now Bent's Old Fort National Historic Site outside Las Animas.
Bent's Fort;; CHS WPA 378, Report on Expedition off the Canadian River. William Bent; CHS F-2.

Top & left: This 1845 depiction of Bent's Fort by J.W. Abert shows the bastion during its most important period. Established in 1834 by brothers William and Charles Bent along with

Right: Freed slave and frontiersman Jim Beckwourth worked at Bent's Fort. Later, he started his own business, founding "El Pueblo" in 1842 near the confluence of the Arkansas River and

Fountain Creek. His trading post for dry goods and powerful "Taos Lightning" whiskey eventually evolved into the city of Pueblo.
James Beckwourth; CHS F-17954.

Bottom: Casimiro Barela moved from New Mexico to Colorado in 1847, homesteading near Trinidad. Ranching and freighting made him a wealthy man and eventually he entered politics, serving on the territorial legislature and later as a state senator from Las Animas County. Throughout his career he worked to protect the interests of Colorado's poorly-represented Hispanic community.
Casimiro Barela; CHS F-32689.

Top: Hispanics from New Mexico were the first settlers in Colorado, establishing ranches and farms along the Arkansas River and in the San Luis Valley. In 1851, Colorado's first permanent Hispanic community was founded at the town of San Luis.
Hispanic Ranch; CHS F 33148.

SAND CREEK MASSACRE

White Antelope chanted his death song, "Only the mountains live forever" on November 29, 1864.

The Southern Cheyenne warrior was encamped along the Big Sandy (later called Sand Creek) in southeastern Colorado. The village included some 500 inhabitants, mostly Southern Cheyenne lead by Chief Black Kettle, and a small band of Arapaho under Chief Left Hand. The two leaders had brought their people here in the belief that they were under the protection of U.S. authorities.

In September of the same year, Black Kettle and other chiefs had met with Colorado's Governor John Evans and Colonel John M. Chivington, the commander of the Colorado Military District, at Camp Weld near Denver. Major Edward W. Wynkoop, the commander of Fort Lyon, had arranged the meeting to resolve recent conflicts between settlers, soldiers and various Plains Indian peoples.

Having lived near the tribespeople for some time, Wynkoop had earned their trust and respect. Indeed, they knew him as "Tall Chief." Wynkoop once remarked that among the Natives, he felt as though he were "in the presence of superior beings." He hoped that the Camp Weld conference would bring peace between the aboriginal people he admired and the white people he represented. The meeting ended with a tacit understanding that the Cheyenne and Arapaho would cease hostilities and submit to U.S. military authority. After gathering at Fort Lyon, they were instructed to take up camp near Sand Creek.

SAND CREEK MASSACRE

Edward Wynkoop

Colonel John Chivington

Chivington had other plans, however. The War Department had authorized the formation of the Third Regiment of Colorado Volunteers to "pursue, kill, and destroy all hostile Indians that infest the plains." With a peaceful agreement so close at hand, however, Denver newspapers began to refer to Chivington's new regiment as the "Bloodless Third."

By late November, Chivington, along with a 1,000 troops, arrived at Fort Lyon, which was now under the command of Major Scott J. Anthony. On the evening of November 27, the military contingent left the fort for Sand Creek. At dawn the next morning, Chivington ordered his men to open fire on the sleeping village. When the battle ended around noon, more than 150 Cheyenne and Arapaho lay dead, including many women and children. The now "Bloody Thirdsters" collected scalps and later displayed them at a Denver theater.

Wynkoop was stationed at Fort Riley, Kansas, when news of the massacre reached him. Reports indicate that he was, "wild with rage when he heard of the crime committed by Chivington and his men, and demanded their trial and punishment for the deed." War Department and Congressional investigations did occur, but no charges were ever brought against Chivington or any of his soldiers.

Photos: Edward Wynkoop; CHS F-1893. Colonel John Chivington; CHS F-22. Sand Creek Massacre; CHS F-40341, Robert Lindneux painting.

OURAY

Historical accounts vary as to the early life of the great Ute leader, Ouray, whose name translates simply to "Arrow." Some say he was born in Colorado, while others contend that Taos, New Mexico, was his birthplace. Both 1820 and 1833 have been listed as the year of his birth. The latter is supported by scholars who believe the claim that stars fell from heaven at Ouray's birth, a sure sign of his greatness. The year 1833 witnessed unusually heavy meteor showers coming from the constellation Leo.

Ouray's father is said to have been a Ute chief and his mother a Jicarilla Apache. Certainly he was raised in the Ute tradition, but perhaps learned to speak English and Spanish while living with a family near Taos. With the death of his father, Ouray assumed the leadership of the Uncompahgre, one of the seven tribal bands comprising the Ute nation.

He is said to have only been 17 when he inherited the responsibility of tribal leadership. Over the course of his long career, he rose to the challenge. In the late 1800s, Chief Ouray's eloquence and insight guided a generation of Utes through the most difficult period of their history.

His language skills and cool-headed demeanor earned the respect of U.S. government negotiators. Ouray participated in every major Ute treaty put forth by Washington D.C. His opinion and approval were essential to white officials and politicians, who regarded him as the leader of all Utes. Ouray's sage voice had considerable influence with the other Ute bands; he often assuaged their anger at the thoughtless incursions of fortune-seekers and settlers.

Sadly, his determined efforts couldn't forestall the inevitable deportation of Utes from their homeland. Ouray himself, however, was spared this final indignity. Shortly after the conclusion of the agreement which forced all Utes onto reservations in Utah and southern Colorado, Ouray died. In keeping with Ute custom, his body was wrapped in blankets and buried in secret.

Photos: Ouray; CHS F-1075 WPA 1063S. Ute Delegation to Washington 1880; CHS F-7100, Panel #2..

THE MEEKER MASSACRE

NATHAN MEEKER got his start in Colorado while leading the founding of Greeley on the Front Range. In 1878, he became an Indian Agent at the White River Agency on the Western Slope with a goal to "Americanize" the Utes into farmers. Long accustomed to a nomadic hunting and gathering lifestyle, the Utes didn't easily take to agrarian ways. Meeker's stern demeanor and wholesale disregard for Ute customs and values quickly alienated the people he was charged with helping.

During the summer of 1879, many of the Utes abandoned the reservation. Those who stayed found Meeker unrepentant in his oppressive pursuit to "civilize" them. When Meeker ordered the plowing of their horse-racing field and pastures, the Utes had had enough.

Fearing imminent reprisal, Meeker called for troops, and Major Thomas T. Thornburgh was dispatched with a small force of men. The Utes learned of the approaching cavalry, went into action and surprised Thornburgh's unit at Mill Creek. In the skirmish, Thornburgh was killed along with 13 soldiers. Enraged, the Utes next pursued Meeker himself, killing him and 11 other men at the White River Indian Agency. Meeker's wife, Avilla, his daughter, Josephine, and a Mrs.

But don't forget to patronize the Pioneer Grocery of Colorado.
WOLFE LONDONER.

Shadrack Price and her two children were abducted and held captive for more than a month on Grand Mesa before they were released.

The government's response to the incident echoed the cry of the newspapers: "The Utes Must Go." In 1880, Chief Ouray and other Ute leaders reluctantly agreed to forsake their verdant valleys and forests for dusty reservations in Utah and extreme southern Colorado.

Photos: Meeker Massacre; CHS Engraving of Miss Meeker #24, 203 WPA. Utes Must Go Newspaper Graphic; CHS F-44177.

Opposite: These Ute children, photographed in the late 1800s, would never know their traditional homelands or customs. After the Meeker Massacre and resulting Ute deportation, many Ute children were forced to attend boarding schools run similar to the military, subjecting pupils to uniforms, drills and duties.
Indian Children; CHS 5718 WHJ Indians Notebook.

Bottom: A Ute delegation, escorted by Indian agents, was invited to the lavish National Mining and Industrial Exposition held in Denver during the summer of 1882. The exhibition extolled the immense mineral riches of Colorado. Ironically, these treasures were mostly contained on lands that were forfeited by the Utes in a series of treaties. The Utes were asked to attend the exposition to perform a war dance.
Denver 1882 National Mining Exposition; CHS F-42387.

Top: In July of 1858, a sharp-eyed prospector from the state of Georgia—William Green Russell—churned up gold flakes along the banks of Little Dry Creek, near the confluence of Cherry Creek and the South Platte River. By November, two mining camps straddled the banks of the South Platte River: Auraria on the west, St. Charles on the east. The name Denver wasn't adopted for the combined communities until 1859, about the same time this photograph was taken.
Denver Wagon Train; CHS F-21970.

Pikes Peak or Bust

*S*avvy prospectors had always suspected that Colorado's mountains held mineral riches. Indeed, a few argonauts passed this way en route to the great "California Gold Rush" of 1849, but they didn't stay. "California here I come," was their calling.

Nearly a full decade passed before Georgian miners turned up some Colorado color while panning along the banks of Little Dry Creek, near the confluence of the South Platte River and Cherry Creek. News of the find spread quickly, and before long the rush began. "Pikes Peak or Bust" became the rallying call, though the great mountain lie some 70 miles south from the gold strike. To most would-be prospectors, it was the only known landmark in Colorado.

By the spring of 1859, a rag-tag city which would later be called Denver had taken root on either side of the South Platte River. Denver's gold proved to be insubstantial, and it wasn't long before frustrated prospectors pushed farther into the mountains. Here, they hit pay dirt. Huge strikes along the forks of Clear Creek silenced the naysayers who decried Colorado's mineral wealth as "humbug."

Central City's rise to gilded stardom was nothing short of meteoric. It became "The Richest Square Mile on Earth." But Central City's story would be only one of many Colorado boomtown sagas; miners revealed a mineral belt of gold and silver arcing southwest of Central City, sweeping over the Continental Divide and plunging far into the San Juan Mountains. Georgetown, Silver Plume, Leadville, Aspen, Silverton, Ouray and Cripple Creek all lay in its path.

Mining was the gear upon which Colorado's future revolved well into the turn of the century. Stunning fortunes were made, not only by miners, but also by road builders and railway tycoons, smelter barons and merchant princes eager to cater to the whims of Colorado's nouveau riche. Names such as Nathaniel Hill, William Jackson Palmer, Horace Tabor, Otto Mears, and Thomas Walsh appeared in the newspaper headlines of the day. Their

See page 22

Top: Early prospectors worked Colorado's gold primarily with panning and sluicing, searching for so-called "free" gold: loose dust and flour, nuggets and wires. It was a back-breaking occupation that could quickly yield profits at a good claim, but seldom did free gold exist in such quantities as to make it a long-lasting enterprise. "Gypsy miners" were skilled at pitching camp, working a claim until it played out, then moving on to the next likely area when the "pickin's got slim." *Miner with Pan; CHS F-461.*

Bottom: "Pikes Peak or Bust" became the rallying call of gold-hungry "59ers," those hardy souls who trekked to Colorado's Front Range mining region in 1859. It is estimated that as many as 100,000 people heeded the call to the goldfields. No more than 40,000 actually made it to Denver, and of them, only about 2,000 stayed until 1860. Many of those intrepid prospectors went bust. Denver's gold reserves were meager at best. *Pikes Peak or Bust Wagon; CHS.*

stories of fame, fortune and sometimes failure, would become Colorado legends.

Politicians easily succumbed to the mesmerizing glimmer of Colorado's gold and silver. Statehood would come in 1876, not soon enough for some of the territory's early Republican-minded boosters, but timely indeed for the election of Republican President Rutherford B. Hayes. Still, the state's influence couldn't forestall the worldwide drop in silver prices and the devastating 1893 repeal of the Sherman Silver Purchase Act, which guaranteed silver's high value by U.S. government procurement commitments.

Colorado's boom times began to bust, and had it not been for two spectacular gold discoveries, the state's overall financial future would have looked bleak. Cripple Creek's "Bowl of Gold" and the San Juan's gold-embedded tellurium finds propped up Colorado's mining economy well into the early 20th century. Estimates value the take at Cripple Creek alone at well over $600 million. But, by the end of World War I, the brightest fortunes of Pikes Peak and the San Juans had dulled, as had those of the "Centennial State's" other mining towns.

Opposite: When noted journalist and editor Horace Greeley visited Denver in July, 1859, he described it as a "log city of 150 dwellings, not three-fourths completed nor one-third fit to be." This view of Denver's Larimer Street taken sometime after October, 1862, depicts how rapidly Denver had progressed. Less than two years after Greeley's inspection, the frontier metropolis boasted a prosperous-looking downtown with brick buildings and a post office. The days of tent saloons and cobbled-together houses were quickly fading from the landscape and from memory. *Larimer Street Mule Train; CHS F-4082.*

Top: Although Denver survived a devastating fire in April, 1863, it was the flood of May, 1864 which nearly wiped the town off the territorial map. A wall of water raged down Cherry Creek taking eight known victims in addition to the City Hall, the Methodist Church and the office of the *Rocky Mountain News. Cherry Creek Flood 1864; CHS F-26642.*

Above: Gold dust was the chief currency during Colorado's early mining days. However, it proved to be a tiresome monetary unit—difficult to value and handle, and risky to ship across the vast unprotected territory. Several private mints—an allowable enterprise back then—stepped in to help assuage the problem. A Leavenworth banking concern, Clark, Gruber & Company, was one of the most successful. For a time it cast its own $2.50, $5 and $20 gold pieces and later, it issued scrip for use by the local populace. In 1863, the U.S. federal government acquired the company's operations, using its facilities primarily as an assay office. The Denver Mint wasn't established until 1906. *Clark, Gruber & CO. Money: CHS F-2098.*

As this battered battle flag testifies, the "Stars and Stripes" prevailed as Silbey's forces were stopped in their march at Glorieta Pass, New Mexico. A combined force of Union soldiers under Colonel Edward R. Canby and First Regiment of Colorado Infantry lead by John Slough routed the Confederates at what has been called the "Gettysburg of the West." *U.S. Flag; CHS.*

Bottom: At the end of the Civil War many veterans on both sides of the conflict were ready for a new life. Tales of Colorado's mineral riches lured ex-soldiers to become overnight prospectors, many arriving with only the essentials, still wearing the uniforms of their battle days.
Confederate Soldier/Miner; CHS F-17853.

Top: Although the Civil War was largely fought in the eastern U.S., western territories nonetheless found themselves embroiled in the "War Between the States." A Confederate Texan army under the command of General Henry S. Sibley swept through the Southwest, eyeing the wealth of Colorado's gold fields.

AUNT CLARA BROWN—BLACK PIONEER

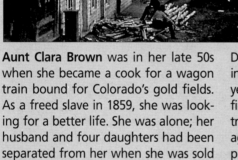

Aunt Clara Brown was in her late 50s when she became a cook for a wagon train bound for Colorado's gold fields. As a freed slave in 1859, she was looking for a better life. She was alone; her husband and four daughters had been separated from her when she was sold to a new master in 1835.

Arriving in Denver, Brown worked in a bakery until she could arrange passage to Central City. She had heard that miners didn't care much for washing and ironing, two skills Brown possessed. In Central City she rented a ramshackle cabin and opened a laundry. Business flourished and Brown was frugal. Within a few years, she acquired property, mining claims, and put aside money.

At the end of the Civil War, Brown traveled to Tennessee, where she used her good fortune to help recently freed slaves relocate to Colorado. The 1863 Cherry Creek flood destroyed proof of her Denver holdings, and 10 years later a fire at Central City ravaged other property. In 1880, nearly destitute, she returned to Denver to live in a small house on Arapahoe Street.

Two years later, Brown, age 82, ailing and unable to earn a living, received word that one of her daughters, Eliza Jane, was living in Council Bluffs, Iowa. Despite her frailty and poverty, Brown set out from Denver on her last trip back East. After nearly 50 years, she finally embraced a daughter cruelly taken from her so many years ago.

Photos: Central City; CHS F-11480. Aunt Clara Brown; CHS F-3714.

NATHANIEL HILL'S SMELTER

As early as 1864, rumors were circulating that Colorado's rich gold finds were already history. A mere five years had passed since the mineral's discovery, yet placer miners had succeeded in panning, sluicing and dredging through most of the "free" gold: loose dust and flour, nuggets and wire.

Free gold also exists in "lodes," veins and rivulets of ore trapped within quartz and other rock. Hardrock mining with picks, shovels and dynamite required more work and tested the technology of the day, as gold had to be separated from its worthless amalgam. Various techniques, such as crushing and chemical baths, were employed on the composite rock, but none yielded an efficient and profitable process.

Enter Nathaniel Hill. As a professor of chemistry at Brown University, Hill understood the miners' problem. In 1865, he made his first trip to the Rockies to study the situation. He also traveled to Swansea, Wales to see how Europeans dealt with ore reduction, even shipping 70 tons of Central City diggings there for experimental processing.

By 1868, Hill had devised an improved extraction process for the low-grade ore surfacing at Central City. Backed by New England capitalists, the Boston and Colorado Smelting Company opened in nearby Black Hawk with immediate success. Ore was subjected to intense firing in reverberatory furnaces, which separated worthless slag from a copper matte infused with gold and silver. These composite plates were then shipped to Swansea for further refining into their constituent metals. Later, this final process was relocated to Hill's Colorado plant.

Hill was hailed as a hero to hard-rock miners, and was rewarded handsomely with the profits of his smelting works. He stayed in Colorado and later entered politics, serving as a U.S. Senator from 1879 to 1885.

Photos: Nathaniel Hill; CHS F-44158. Black Hawk Smelter; CHS F-10396.

Opposite: Railroads raced to reach newly discovered mining camps. Enticing profits from hauling freight, ore and passengers tempted railroad barons to lay tracks far into Colorado's alpine terrain. By 1896, Colorado had more than 4,700 miles of track operated by 15 railroads, employing some 12,000 workers.

To reach the mining regions, Herculean efforts were often required. Steep mountain passes posed formidable problems for railroad design and construction, as did natural obstructions. Railroads such as the Colorado Midland chiseled stupendous tunnels, like this one outside Manitou Springs looking toward Cameron Cone, to secure their lumbering cars' progress through the Rocky Mountains. *Train Tunnel; CHS F-28441.*

Top: To overcome the nearly eight percent grade from Georgetown to Silver Plume, the Colorado Central Railroad installed a "loop." Essentially, it sent trains on a corkscrew course up the valley and over spindly Devil's Gate Viaduct, strung 100 feet above Clear Creek. In total, locomotives and cars were lifted more than 600 feet in elevation by the time they pulled into Silver Plume some two miles away.

Tracks were "narrow gauge," meaning the distance between rails was three feet rather than the "standard gauge" of four feet, eight and one-half inches. Narrow gauge tracks considerably improved the turning radius which trains could negotiate and therefore cut overall construction costs in the mountains from $90,000 per mile to approximately $20,000 per mile. *Georgetown Loop; CHS F-11252, WHJ Collection.*

of plows to the front of loco-motives. One of the most popular was a steam-driven rotary plow with giant blades that munched through snow, throwing great heaps aside as the train slowly bulldozed forward.
Train & Snow; CHS Buckwalter #737.

Top: Construction challenges were but one of many adversities that plagued early railroad operators. The Rocky Mountains' terrain lived up to its name; frequent rock slides and avalanches caused numerous train wrecks. Below Battle Mountain near present-day Vail, the tracks of the Denver and Rio Grande Railroad snaked through eight tortuously curved miles of the Eagle River Canyon. Victims of derailments e waited hours for relief trains.
Train Wreck; CHS 1-D2-Cat#62. H.W. Luby Collection.

Opposite: The Colorado Midland Railroad, shown here traversing Hell Gate west of Leadville with three locomotives, began in 1886 as a standard-gauge line from Colorado Springs to the West Coast. It only made it as far as Grand Junction before it connected with the rails of the Rio Grande Western. The Midland's route crossed through some of Colorado's most dramatic scenery, making it one of the most popular tourist trains of the time. Nonetheless, rev-enue failed to keep the train on a prosperous financial track. The Midland ceased operations in 1921, recording at the time the largest single railroad failure in America.
Colorado Midland; CHS F-3487.

Bottom: For railroads traversing the Colorado high country, furious winter storms often hampered travel with immense snowdrifts, sometimes taller than the train itself. To clear the routes, trains attached various types

COLORADO STATEHOOD

Statehood recognition did not come easily to Colorado. Various federal and local political factions disputed the territory's legislative issue for almost 15 years. In the end, Colorado's change of status was as much a result of the upcoming 1876 presidential election as the desire of local citizens for full representation in the United States.

Republican President Ulysses S. Grant was ending his second term and the Republican Party's chosen replacement for him was Rutherford B. Hayes, who faced stiff opposition from Democratic candidate hopeful Samuel Tilden.

Colorado was staunchly Republican and, if granted statehood, could contribute three Republican-oriented electoral votes to the election. Consequently, President Grant lost no time in proclaiming Colorado a state on August 1, 1876, shortly before the pending election. That autumn, Hayes was chosen to be the 19th U.S. president, besting Tilden by only one electoral vote. Clearly, Colorado's ballot contribution helped win the day. The year 1876 also marked the centennial of the nation and, therefore, Colorado became the "Centennial State."

Painter Joseph Hitchins commemorated the occasion in 1884 with his *Admission of Colorado to the Union*. In the scene, an angel trumpets the moment as Senator Jerome B. Chaffee escorts the demur white-gowned Miss Colorado to meet the regal Madame Columbia. Standing to the left of Miss Colorado is Representative James Belford, a firm supporter of Colorado's entrance into statehood. *Rocky Mountain News* founder and editor, William Byers, proudly holds a copy of his newspaper, while white-bearded John Evans, Colorado's second territorial governor, looks on approvingly from the back row.

Photo: Colorado Statehood Painting; CHS F-24289.

Top: While there is little evidence that children worked in the hard-rock gold and silver mines, youngsters were occasionally pressed into pick-and-shovel service at coal mines. Mining paid relatively high wages; in 1881, coal miners took home 75 cents per ton and gold and silver miners made $2 to $3 a day, compared to wages of railroad workers at $1.50 to $2.50 per day, or wood choppers at $1.10 per cord. *Kid Miners; CHS F-31655.*

Bottom: By the early 1870s, the area around California Gulch seemed played out to most miners. Free gold had been the primary interest, and in large measure it had all been panned and sluiced up. What was left were tons of carbonate ore, potentially rich in silver but too expensive to work without on-site smelters. When the St. Louis Smelting and Refining Company established the Harrison Reduction Works on Carbonate Hill, it spawned silver production and the community of Leadville. Workers flowed in and by 1877, Leadville was a dusty, treeless town of some 2,000 shanties, along with 115 gambling houses, 120 saloons and 35 brothels. *Leadville; CHS Buckwalter Book II #59.*

RAGS TO RICHES TO RAGS: THE TABORS

Augusta Tabor   Horace Tabor   Baby Doe

No name better epitomizes the booms and busts of Colorado's mining era than that of Horace Austin Warner Tabor. His story, and that of his two wives, reads like the script of a Victorian melodrama.

The tale begins in faraway Vermont, where Tabor worked as a stonecutter. There, he married the bosses' daughter, Augusta, and soon the two left the backbreaking business to seek their fortune out West. The newlyweds homesteaded in Kansas before heading into Colorado's gold country during the early days of the "Pikes Peak or Bust Gold Rush." Prospecting failed to sustain them, yet they persevered. Augusta transformed their shacks into boarding houses, while Horace became a merchant, supplying goods to miners who hadn't yet given up on finding that elusive "Mother Lode."

Oro City, later Leadville, became their home in 1868. It was here that Lady Luck finally smiled upon the Tabors. As was the custom, Tabor agreed to grubstake a couple of prospectors with supplies in return for a one-third interest in their unproved mine. It was the best deal Tabor ever made. The "Little Pittsburgh" paid off quickly, producing $20,000 of ore per week. Within a year, Tabor sold his share for a $1 million.

Wealth beget more wealth for Tabor. He plowed his windfall into a dozen schemes: shares of other profitable mines, grand hotels and opera houses. In Denver, he built a mansion suitable for a "Silver King," and soon tried his hand at politics. Money and power became Tabor's mistresses, while dutiful Augusta faded from the spotlight of her husband's dazzling new life.

Then Tabor met Elizabeth McCourt Doe, better known as "Baby Doe." She was a divorcée, a stunning beauty with "a complexion so clear that it reminds one of the rose blush mingling with the pure white lily." Augusta soon received a plea for divorce and a settlement of $300,000. When Tabor was sent to Washington D.C. in 1883 to serve a 30-day term as one of Colorado's U.S. Senators, he wed Baby Doe amidst a glittering

RAGS TO RICHES TO RAGS: THE TABORS

years followed as the Tabors floundered further into poverty. In 1898, influential friends rescued the family by securing Tabor's appointment as Denver's postmaster. Tabor diligently performed his duties, but within a year, he fell ill and died.

Throughout Tabor's fall from glory he had retained ownership of the "Matchless Mine" in Leadville. It had played out years ago, but Tabor always believed it would produce again one day. So strong was his conviction, that supposedly on his deathbed he swore Baby Doe to a promise: "Never sell the Matchless."

Baby Doe honored her husband's last request. She moved into a tool shed behind the Matchless and for the next three decades patched together a meager and obscure existence. Acquaintances found the recluse frozen to death in March, 1935.

Ironically, Augusta died a wealthy women. She invested her divorce settlement wisely, and gained a reputation as one of Colorado's best mining authorities—a truly notable achievement in a time when a woman's business acumen seldom received praise.

Photos: Horace Tabor; CHS 192 WPA. Augusta Tabor, CHS by A.E. Rinehart. Baby Doe Tabor, CHS F-31397. Baby Doe Tabor and cabin; CHS F-30239.

spectacle. The bride's dress alone cost $7,000 and her diamond necklace, $90,000. Guests included the rich and famous, including President Chester A. Arthur. Many of the attendees' wives failed to grace the occasion; it was simply too scandalous.

For a decade, the Tabors lived in bliss, despite scorn by Denver society and Horace's failed campaigns to win a U.S. Senate seat in 1886 and the Colorado governorship in 1888. Two daughters, Rosemary Silver Dollar Echo and Elizabeth Pearl, kept the household cheerful. Tabor's financial empire continued to burgeon, though increasingly, speculative mining stocks rather than hard assets formed his investment portfolio.

The repeal of the Sherman Silver Purchase Act in 1893 closed the book on the Tabors' fairytale. Almost overnight, their fortune soured forcing the them to liquidate their gilded trappings. Gone were the mansions and stables, furs and diamonds. Lean

Top: Otto Mears eased the isolation of the mining camps in the San Juan Mountains. Over the span of 20 years, he financed the construction of nearly 300 miles of toll roads connecting Silverton, Ouray and Lake City. Perilous in places, the roads were nonetheless functional, carrying passengers, goods and supplies for the prospering mining industry. This photograph shows the toll station at Bear Creek Falls between Ouray and Ironton.
Bear Creek Toll Station; CHS Buckwalter Collection.

Bottom: Born in Russia in 1840, Mears spent time in the California mining areas before coming to southern Colorado in 1865. Initially, he earned a living by operating a gristmill and sawmill at Conejos. He then progressed to road building and later, to railroad construction, financing the Rio Grande Southern Railroad. By 1892, Mears created a southern Colorado transportation empire.
Otto Mears; CHS F-1254.

ALFERD THE CANNIBAL

Alferd (not Alfred) Packer stumbled out of a blizzard in 1873 at the Los Piños Indian Agency near present-day Lake City in the San Juan Mountains. He said he'd been left behind by his five companions on their journey from an encampment near Delta to Los Piños.

Oddly, despite six weeks "alone" atop a blizzard-swept mountain range, Packer didn't appear the least bit gaunt. And why was he packing so much cash?

The gruesome answers came when five bodies turned up in August—picked clean. Here's the story as Packer told it: The party of five men—Packer, Frank Miller, James Humphrey, Israel Swan, George Noon and Wilson Bell—got lost about 10 days into their excursion. When Swan died they diced and devoured him. Next they served up Humphrey, then Miller. Packer swore that while he was away hunting game, Bell murdered Noon and came after him with a hatchet. In self-defense, Packer killed Bell.

The jury at his first trial, held nearly 10 years later, believed otherwise. They found him guilty of murder. Judge Melville B. Gerry, delivering a sentence destined for Colorado folklore, has been reported as saying:

"*Stand up, yah voracious man-eatin' SOB and receive your sintince! There was seven Democrats in Hinsdale County and yah et five of thim! I sintince you to be hanged by th' neck ontil yer dead, dead, dead, as a warnin' ag'in reducin' the Democratic population...ye Republican cannibal!*"

Packer didn't hang; he was sentenced to 40 years in prison but was eventually released.

Photos: Skeletons; CHS, Murder Victims from Harper's Weekly 1874. Packer; CHS F-3823.

Opposite Top: Creede was the last of the San Juan Mountain's "Silver Queens." Mines were first tapped in 1889, only four years before the repeal of the Sherman Silver Purchase Act, which melted down silver prices as well as the silver mining industry. Still, during its brilliant moment Creede turned out more than 80 tons of silver. Due to its proximity to existing railroad lines and the relative ease of negotiating Slumgullion Pass, Creede was more accessible than many other mining towns. The settlement soon overflowed with prospectors and the usual retinue of gamblers and dance hall girls ready to help lucky miners spend their fortunes.
Creede Streets; CHS F-4231 WHJ Cities Notebook.

Opposite Bottom: In its silver-mining heyday, Silverton was dubbed "the mining town that never quit." Situated in a high valley amidst a ring of 13,000-foot-high San Juan peaks, carousing went on day and night. Lawman Bat Masterson was invited to rid Silverton of its more notorious citizens. It's said that Masterson was so feared that he never once had to draw his gun during the 15 years he lived in Colorado—his quick-draw, sharp-shooter reputation alone kept the peace.
Silverton Overview; CHS F-6165 WHJ Cities Notebook.

Top: During the winter 1879, a few foolhardy miners strapped long ski-like contraptions onto their heavy boots and schussed west from Leadville, crossing the Continental Divide, to slide down into the upper reaches of the Roaring Fork River Valley. They found what they had hoped for—silver-laden carbonate ore.

Within months, a string of mining camps was founded, the most well known becoming Aspen, a clear contender for Colorado's "Silver Capital" title. By 1892, Aspen held 12,000 residents, trailing only Leadville and Denver in population. The Sherman Silver Purchase Act repeal crippled the town, eliminating jobs by the thousands. By 1894, Aspen supported less than 2,000 people. Locals, like W.W. Gormley (pictured here with trained elk pulling his carriage), displayed a certain eccentricity that is still a hallmark of Aspen citizenry.
Aspen with Elk; CHS F-1150.

HARD LUCK MINING

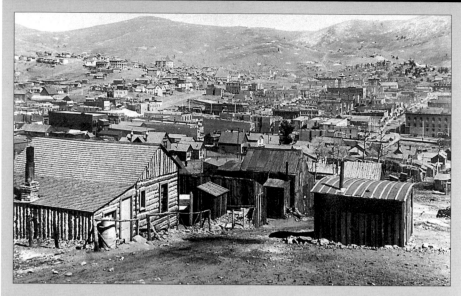

Poor luck has always been a miner's unwelcome companion, and Bob Womack had more than his share of bad acquaintances.

For years, Womack, a cowpoke with the Broken Box Ranch near Cripple Creek, had picked through the extinct volcano crater on the south side of Pikes Peak searching for gold. Everyone thought he was crazy; the terrain of rumpled hills didn't look like gold country. Womack persisted, having occasionally come across rocks and pebbles that showed color. In 1891, he staked a claim called "Poverty Gulch."

A Colorado Springs carpenter, Winfield Scott, heard of Womack's claim and decided to stake one for himself on July 4, 1891, calling it "The Independence." The name was a good choice, and soon Scott became Cripple Creek's first millionaire—footloose and fancy free.

Womack, however, hadn't hit paydirt and parted with his claim, selling it for $300. He gave up too soon. "Poverty Gulch" was anything but poor; it later produced more than $5 million worth of gold.

Photos: Cripple Creek; CHS Jackson Notebook. Bob Womack; CHS F-7666.

Top: Hard-working miners also played hard: some drank, some womanized, most gambled. Favorite games of chance included three-card Monte, a type of shell game, and Faro, a bingo-like pastime, in addition to blackjack, stud poker and roulette. Fortunes were won and lost at places such as Central City's Shoo Fly, Creede's Orleans Club, Leadville's Texas House and Black Hawk's Crook's Palace.

Indeed, Colorado's rough-and-tumble mining camps attracted a good number of swindlers and con men, none more notorious than Soapy Smith. As his name implies, Smith gained a reputation for his slippery dealings with soap. To the amazement of onlookers, Smith would wrap a pile of soapcakes, adding $100 bills to a few of them, then invite members of the audience to purchase bars for $5. The lucky ones—always Smith's cronies—walked away with a clean profit, while others simply ended up with a very expensive bar of soap.

Alice Ivers or "Poker Alice," a she was better known, was as slick as Soapy, only with more class. A widow, Alice turned to gambling to make ends meet, drifting from town to town wherever there resided a gambling house. Packing a gun and chomping a cigar, she outbluffed many a man, often scooping up $1000 a night in winnings.

Although many Colorado mining towns took it upon themselves to outlaw gambling within their districts, an overall state ban on wagering wasn't initiated until 1915. In 1990, Colorado voters approved the establishment of low-stakes ($5 maximum bet) gambling for three historic mining towns: Central City, Black Hawk and Cripple Creek. Gambling is also permitted on the reservations of the Ute Mountain Ute and Southern Ute tribes. *Gambling; CHS F-11890.*

Denver of the 1890s displayed a wealth of classic government buildings and prosperous businesses in this northwest-looking view of 16th Street taken by photographer William Henry Jackson from the state capital's rotunda. *Denver Panorama; CHS F-1628; Denver 1890s, specify panoram*

UNSINKABLE MOLLY

Leadville was a rough-and-ready mining outpost drunk on silver lust when Margaret (Molly) Tobin of Missouri arrived in town. A hard-working Irish Catholic lass filled with spunk, she took odd jobs until she married James Brown, who had a one-eighth share in the "Little Johnny." The mine's wealth proved to be immense, making the Browns' fractional holding worth millions.

In time, the couple moved to Denver and bought a lavish home on Pennsylvania Street in the heart of one of the city's most stylish neighborhoods. Molly soon set her sights on breaking into Denver's fussy high society, at that time lorded over by a close-knit few known as the "Sacred 36." Despite her wealth, the upper crust saw Molly as too low-born and too interested in liberal causes, and they rebuked her social advances.

In a twist of fate, Molly was a passenger on the *Titanic*'s ill-fated maiden voyage, but survived the ordeal by escaping in lifeboat number 6. In the midst of the panic, Molly browbeat the helmsman into action, rallied the terrified survivors and even shared her $60,000 chinchilla coat with her mates. Newspapers of the day lauded her as a heroine. From that day forward, Molly's celebrity status opened the doors of Denver's begrudging élite.

Sadly, Molly's fortunes took a plunge after the death of her husband and a bitter lawsuit over his two wills. Her riches dwindled, but not her style. She was forever outspoken, crusading on behalf of women's suffrage rights and giving generously to worthy causes. Molly died in New York in 1932.

Photo: Margaret Brown; CHS F-4715.

Go West, Young Man

"*G*o West, young man, and grow with the country," was the admonition of New York *Tribune* editor Horace Greeley. The newspaperman was a powerful voice in the nation. What he wrote about his visit to Colorado in 1859 influenced many to try their luck in the new frontier.

Even before gold's discovery in Colorado, farmers and ranchers had begun to settle along the Arkansas River bottomlands and in the San Luis Valley. The wave of gold and silver rushes brought in their wake a rising demand for fresh produce and meat to supply mining camps. Colorado's great prairies became cattle country.

Soon though, "nesters" became the bane of cattle drovers. Farmers dug ditches and fenced in the land, cutting off cattle trails. Inevitably, the competing interests clashed, sometimes violently. In the end, homesteaders spread farther and farther into the range. The glory days of cattle drives and roundups came and went within 30 years.

Colorado's untamed acreage did not easily relinquish its agricultural bounty.

Water was key: this was the so-called "Great American Desert." Collective farming became the answer. Beginning in the 1870s, "colonies" cropped up. Individual sodbusters pooled their resources to build dams, irrigation canals and agricultural centers to serve an entire community. The markets for farmers' produce expanded as Colorado became more industrialized. Railroad tracks and smelters followed the mining booms, each requiring thousands of workers. Immigrants from around the world flowed into the land of opportunity.

By 1900, Colorado held some 500,000 residents and surpassed the national population growth average. The early part of the 20th century would feel the effect of those growing pains. Fierce labor disputes would pit workers' rights against the interests of big business. Natural disasters—floods, crop failures and dust storms—further tested the resolve of Coloradans as the state weathered the Great Depression.

Photo opposite: Young cowboy; CHS F-34015, Dean Photo Grand Junction.

Opposite Top: The demand for fresh beef in mining camps spurred the development of Colorado's cattle-ranching industry. Further, a combination of factors—the end of the Civil War, a cattle glut in Texas and the introduction of rail service at Denver—lured wranglers on long cattle drives into Colorado to ship range-fed cattle to beef-starved northeastern markets.

Routes such as the Goodnight-Loving Trail, blazed by Charles Goodnight and Oliver Loving, came north through New Mexico and skirted the Front Range into Denver, where feed lots held the cattle for shipment. Cattle barons settled on the Eastern Plains, amassing thousands of head of cattle, which grazed on the grassland that once fed bison. In 1867, the Colorado Territory contained less than 150,000 cattle, but within eight years that number had swelled to nearly 500,000.
Cowboy Lineup; CHS F-7909.

Opposite Bottom: While most cattle roundups were rather small—usually a dozen men for a herd of 3,000— occasional regional roundups required as many as 500 cowboys, 3,500 horses and 50 chuckwagons. In 1880, cattle in Colorado sold for an average of $14.50 per head, and it cost less than a $1 per head (including cowpoke wages) to herd a string of cattle from Texas, where beef sold for less than $10 per head. Clearly, cattle drives could be profitable ventures.
Cowboys at Rest; CHS F-3519, Camp Stool Outfit.

Top: Everyone pitched in to survive in the unforgiving ranching business. The Becker sisters of the San Luis Valley demonstrate in this photograph that cowgirls branded cattle with the best of cowboys. In the state's wide open ranges, cattle branding was essential to identify strays and thwart rustlers. As early as 1867, the Colorado Stockgrowers Association formed to record brands and nurture the industry.
Cowgirls Branding; CHS F-5441.

CONQUERING THE GREAT AMERICAN DESERT

By the 1860s, farmers were already settled in the fertile bottomlands of Colorado's Arkansas, South Platte and Rio Grande river valleys, yet the prospect of a large-scale agrarian industry looked bleak. The land beyond the rivers was simply too arid, hence its designation as the "Great American Desert."

Farmers suspected that if they could just get enough water to the Colorado prairie, the land would yield a bounty of grain and produce. However, the task of constructing dams, headgates and irrigation canals to siphon water from the rivers would require substantial investment and teamwork. This would be the work of "colonies."

The colony or "collective" farming concept had been tried and proved successful at numerous locations in the Midwest and East. Essentially, it called for like-minded individuals to pool together their meager resources. Cohesion was critical to the fledgling communities. Some were conceived as "utopias" where residents drew strength from a common religious or ethnic background, or simply a higher moral purpose. Other colonies were more corporate in nature. "Shareholders" launched enterprises to build town halls, schools, and other community necessities in addition to irrigation facilities.

Colorado's first successful agricultural venture, the Union Colony Association, which later became Greeley, merged the various philoso-phies. It also had an influential proponent.

Horace Greeley was the outspoken editor of the popular New York *Tribune*. Having toured Colorado in 1859, he was convinced that the territory's grassland would support extensive farming if done with a concerted effort. The *Tribune*'s agricultural editor, Nathan C. Meeker, agreed. In 1869, the two men, along with Robert A. Cameron, formed the Union Colony Association with Meeker as president and man-

CONQUERING THE GREAT AMERICAN DESERT

ager. By the spring of the following year, 12,000 acres had been procured, at the confluence of the Cache la Poudre and the South Platte rivers.

For a membership fee of $155, homesteaders received a town lot and farm plot; money left over was spent on public services and digging irrigation canals. Within months, 3,000 families were pulling together in Greeley to create a unified American Dream. By summer's end, the first 10-mile-long canal delivered water to the town. Within a year, some 400 houses, a town hall, a library, a lyceum, schools and churches dotted the prairie. Notably absent were saloons and pool halls; Greeley was a "dry" town, dedicated to "sobriety, good order, peace, harmony, and prosperity."

The town flourished and other colonies soon formed along the Front Range. They were modeled after Greeley in form, if not in spirit; several communities eschewed Greeley's temperance highroad, preferring the solace of the "devil's brew." By 1890, Colorado's Eastern Plains held more than one million irrigated acres.

Photos: Greeley town; CHS F-12017. Nathan Meeker; CHS F-2880. Horace Greeley; CHS F-37405.

Top: For early immigrants to Colorado's prairie and plateaus, sod houses were the ideal instant home. They were relatively easy to build, requiring about a week of hard labor. Using a good "grasshopper plow," a settler cut strips of sod 12 to 14 inches wide and about four inches thick to make sod blocks. Construction of the three-foot-thick walls followed the same methods as laying brick: breaking joints and leveling successive layers offset the inevitable settling and sagging that occurred with time.

What little timber was used, sometimes collected from sparse cottonwood forests miles away, served as supporting beams and rafters, which were covered with willow brush and a blanket of sod to form the roof. With expenses for a small windowpane, lumber for a door and a few nails, the total price for a "soddy" could be as low as $3. Under favorable weather conditions they would last for years.

Although they were mostly seen as temporary dwellings until a proper all-wood house could be afforded, sod houses were nonetheless comfortable. They were well insulated from winter winds and cool during the stifling heat of summer. Many a soddy housewife could also point out a few inconveniences. Sod, whether it lay on the ground or formed a wall, housed countless insects and probing field mice, which in turn were meals for other creatures. Snakes were common uninvited guests as they wriggled in through the roof and walls. Watchful prairie women kept a broom within reach to shoo away slithering intruders.
Sod House; CHS F-44346.

soon wrested control of the company for themselves. *Osgood; CHS F-43689.*

Top: John C. Osgood headed Colorado Fuel and Iron (CF&I), a virtual industrial empire which controlled ore mines, vast coalfields and factories. Osgood envisioned an industrial utopia for his employees with tidy Victorian cottages for families, a clubhouse for his bachelor workers and morale-boosting community services such as a library and theater, even a dairy herd. This vision became the town of Redstone, located near Osgood's coal mines and coking ovens.

Not far from his workers, Osgood built Cleveholm, a 42-room manor on the Crystal River. Interior decoration was fit for a lord: elephant-hide wall coverings, silk brocade furnishings, Persian rugs, richly-colored velvet drapes and hand-carved stone fireplaces. Osgood's wife was known as "Lady Bountiful," for she ensured that during Christmas time, every Redstone child got his or her Santa Claus wish. *Redstone; CHS F-17975.*

Bottom:
When Osgood faced a vicious takeover battle for CF&I from financier E.H. Harriman, he turned to tycoons John D. Rockefeller and George J. Gould for financial backing. The two men rescued Osgood, but

Opposite Top: Schools of the era sought to teach not only the basic skills of reading, writing and arithmetic, but also infuse young minds with a variety of topics that might include subjects such as Ancient Geography, Astronomy, Philosophy, Mythology, Poetry, Prose, Composition and Latin. Immigrant workers knew that their children faced a better life if their hard work paid off and youngsters applied themselves. This Louisville school north of Denver posted the names of children who had demonstrated good conduct, then immortalized the moment with a group photograph. Many of the names are either Italian or Slavic in origin, signifying the ethnic clustering of early Colorado communities.
Good Conduct; CHS F-23564.

Opposite Bottom: Life was tough for Colorado's expanding immigrant population. Poor living conditions and premature death had plagued the state's Hispanic residents for generations. Colorado's money and power were concentrated in the north, and largely controlled by Anglo-Americans who often held racist views toward Colorado's Hispanic south.
Hispanic Funeral; CHS F-43377.

Top: Pueblo was Colorado's second largest city by 1890, with a population approaching 25,000. As home to the major operations of Colorado Fuel and Iron, the city's rapid industrial development demanded cheap labor and thousands of immigrants were desperate for any opportunity. As this 1900 photo shows, many Pueblo residents lived under wretched conditions, often in hovels with no running water or sewage facilities.
Pueblo 1900; CHS F-10422, Jackson Notebook.

Top: By the turn of the century, Colorado's African-American population constituted only two percent of the state's total population, but suffered a death rate that was 20 percent higher than that of whites. Concentrated largely in Denver, Colorado Springs and Pueblo, African Americans enjoyed few civil rights by law, and still fewer in actual practice. Most survived on meager employment as servants and laborers.
Bicyclists; CHS Lillybridge Collection.

Bottom: Fugitive slave Barney Ford arrived at Breckenridge in 1860, filing two mining stakes in the name of a Denver lawyer, as territorial law prohibited blacks from registering claims. The attorney, however, swindled Ford out of his claims. Undaunted, Ford headed to Denver working as a bellboy and a barber before eventually opening successful restaurants and hotels. Ford's financial success opened many doors, but as an African-American he lacked the civil rights enjoyed by Colorado's white population. As early as 1866, Ford began righting this wrong by traveling to Washington D.C. to lobby Congressional leaders to withhold Colorado's statehood until rights for African-Americans were guaranteed. Statehood was indeed postponed, though the lack of civil rights assurances was but one of several political problems that delayed Colorado's admittance to the Union. Organizing the Colored Republican Club, Ford continued his quest for fair and equal treatment for African-Americans. In 1873, he ran for the Territorial Legislature, the first black to ever seek public office in Colorado. He was defeated and it would take another 12 years and countless hours of persuasion before Colorado enacted important anti-discrimination legislation.
Barney Ford; CHS F-6323.

Top: The need for reliable irrigation on Colorado's Western Slope initiated the Gunnison River Tunnel and Uncompahgre Reclamation Project. A five-mile tunnel was bored through hard granite west of Poverty Mesa to drain water from the Gunnison River, which would then flow to the arid reaches of the Uncompahgre Plateau. The massive effort took five years to complete and was dedicated by President William H. Taft in 1909. With assured water, the Western Slope's irrigable land doubled to 600,000 acres heralding an agricultural bonanza.
Gunnison Tunnel; CHS F-1247.

Bottom: The Western Slope's relatively mild climate and abundant water supply from new irrigation sources tempted many farmers to plant fruit orchards. Western Slope apples and peaches quickly became highly-valued and much-appreciated summer produce for Coloradans. Market towns such as Paonia, Fruita, Delta and Montrose bloomed in the bounty of a turn-of-the-century fruit boom.
Apple Picking; CHS F-6390.

Opposite Top: To showcase Colorado's agricultural treasure, farming towns and areas staged festivals such as "Watermelon Day," held at Rocky Ford in southeastern Colorado. Events included not only a magnificent display of locally grown fruits and vegetables, but also inspections of produce-processing plants and sporting exhibitions. These ladies are obviously enjoying their juicy watermelons, despite the danger of stains to their starched finery.
Watermelon Girls; CHS.

Opposite Bottom: Rocky Ford's "Watermelon Day" attracted hundreds of autumn visitors, and dozens of free watermelons were distributed to guests. By the end of the day, the grounds were literally transformed into a garden of rinds, thick with flies and bees eager to sip the last remnants of the delectable feast.
Watermelon Day; CHS F-34647.

Top: Better canning techniques, marketing and shipping ensured that turn-of-the-century Coloradans enjoyed fruits and vegetables year-round. Local grocery stores took considerable pride in artfully displaying the abundance of packaged foods available. It was a considerable improvement over Denver's first days, when mere staples were not only hard to find but exorbitant when available: flour at $15 per 100 pounds; corn at $10 per bushel; potatoes at $15 per bushel; and beef at 40 cents a pound.
Stacked Canned Goods; CHS F-2742, Cornforth, Birks.

THE LUDLOW MASSACRE

To industrialists of the early 1900s, Mary Harris Jones was "the most dangerous woman in America." To workers, she was "Mother Jones," a champion of organized labor. For the better part of 60 years, she tirelessly harangued big business for better employee compensation and working conditions.

Jones arrived in Trinidad, Colorado in September, 1913. The workers' plight she found was appalling: squalid company-sponsored housing, usurious prices at company stores and dangerous work practices.

Days after Jones' arrival, 8,000 workers walked off the job, abandoning the mining camps for tent settlements on the prairie. Jones helped organize their strike, but soon the 83-year-old unionist was tagged a "rabble-rouser," and imprisoned by the Colorado National Guard. Upon her release, she traveled to Washington D.C. to testify before Congress on the condition of Colorado mines.

While federal authorities debated the issue, the standoff between striking workers and coal company executives wore on. Tempers reached the flash point on April 20, 1914, when heavily armed national guard troops, peppered with coal company toughs, moved in for a raid on the Ludlow Station tent colony, 12 miles north of Trinidad. A warning shot erupted into a pitched battle, killing one militiaman and five strikers. Two women and 11 children also perished, suffocating from smoke inhalation while trapped in a cellar beneath a blazing tent. The United Mine Workers called the incident the "Ludlow Massacre."

For the following 10 days, coal camps waged war with the Colorado militia. Finally, President Woodrow Wilson dispatched 1,600 federal troops, disarming both sides of the conflict to end the killing. Negotiations were reinstated, and by December of 1914, a settlement was reached.

Photos: Ludlow Men with Guns; CHS F-38372. Mother Jones; CHS F-33658.

GRIFFITH MURDER

In keeping with the rest of the nation, Colorado rode a wave of reformism during the early years of the 20th century. A generation of Americans rose up to battle government corruption, sordid living and working conditions, and a host of social ills ranging from juvenile delinquency to intoxicating liquor to ignorance.

Denver schoolteacher Emily Griffith took up the cause of educating the masses of immigrants which resided in the "Mile High City." Having served as a deputy state superintendent of schools and as a much-admired teacher at Denver's 24th Street Elementary School, she began a crusade to establish a public opportunity school. Her aim was to provide a free school where working people could come for day or evening classes to learn the basics of reading, writing and arithmetic as well as the fundamentals of the English language.

From the beginning, the Opportunity School was a success. Within the first week of the school's opening in September, 1916, more than 1,400 students enrolled, 100 of whom wished to learn typing. The school only had one typewriter and consequently, pupils worked in shifts on the wonderful gadget. Throughout the 1920s, attendance grew at the institution, recording more than 8,000 annual students by the time of Griffith's retirement as principal in 1933. Griffith had achieved the motto which graced the institution's entrance, "For All Who Wish To Learn."

Sadly, in July of 1947, the aging Griffith was brutally murdered along with her sister, Florence, at their cabin near Pinecliffe, 35 miles northwest of Denver. The two women, found in their bedrooms, had been shot in the head with a .38 caliber pistol. The dinner table had been set for three; chili, mashed potatoes and pie were on the stove. A long-time friend, Fred Lundy, who often dined with the sisters, was also missing. Later, Lundy's car was found with a briefcase inside containing $350 and a cryptic note outlining instructions for the disposition of his body. But, there was no Lundy.

A widespread search for Lundy—dead or alive—ensued, with no results. Finally, in August, two fishermen discovered Lundy's body lodged beneath a rock in South Boulder Creek. His remains showed no sign of bullet wounds, so the Griffith case was deemed a double murder and suicide. Still, doubts remain as to what actually occurred, since the murder weapon was never found and Lundy was known to have owned a .25 caliber pistol, not a .38.

Photo: Emily Griffith; CHS.

Jack Dempsey - the new champion ready for action
Photo I.F.S. from N Moser NY.

concrete. Constructing a fortified final resting place for Buffalo Bill seemed necessary to Denverites since Cody, Wyoming, townsfolk had vowed to send a militia to reclaim the body. They never did, but for a time the Cody American Legion Post offered a $10,000 reward for it.
Buffalo Bill; CHS.

Bottom: President Theodore (Teddy) Roosevelt loved the West and came to Colorado twice during his presidency for hunting expeditions. In this 1901 adventure, Roosevelt and his guide, John Goff, bagged a mountain lion. Roosevelt was also known as a stalwart proponent of conservation and in 1905, he created 14 forest reserves throughout Colorado.
Roosevelt with Cougar; CHS F-43016.

Top: At one time he was called "Kid Blackie," later becoming the "Manassa Mauler," but to folks around the town of Manassa in southern Colorado he was simply Jack— Jack Dempsey. By the time Dempsey was 14 he was roaming Colorado's mining camps throwing barefisted punches for a dollar a fight. At age 26, he got a shot at world heavyweight champion Jess Willard and took the crown in three rounds. From 1919 to 1926 the Manassa Mauler's relentless right hand ruled the ring.
Jack Dempsey; CHS F-1397.

Opposite: Perhaps no other person personified the Wild West more than William Frederick Cody—"Buffalo Bill." When Cody died in Denver on January 10, 1917, the "Old Scout's" passing raised a ruckus over ownership of his body. It seems Cody had specified Cedar Mountain outside Cody, Wyoming, as his preferred spot to spend eternity. However, Denver officials hung on to the famous remains, entombing them atop Lookout Mountain under tons of steel-reinforced

Soldiers at Union Station; CHS #1289 Buckwalter Collection.

Top: In response to the national resolution to declare war on Spain in 1898, Senator Henry Teller of Colorado sponsored an amendment which guaranteed that Cuba would not be annexed once it was wrested from the Spanish dominion. To some people, Teller's action seemed to hinder America's emerging world ambition and Manifest Destiny, but for a westerner like Teller, centralized power, particularly when focused in Washington D.C., only meant trouble.
Spanish-American War/Denver; CHS F-4639.

Opposite: In 1930, Mrs. Anthony Joseph became Colorado's first woman aviator went she went aloft in a glider outside Denver. An audience of several thousand spectators were thrilled with the feat and amazed at Mrs. Joseph's bravery
Woman Flier; CHS, Mrs. Anthony Joseph.

Bottom: Coloradans resolved, like many Americans, to join the "splendid little war with Spain," and citizens from the "Centennial State" enthusiastically volunteered for duty. Theodore Roosevelt's "Rough Riders" who stormed the hills of Cuba included soldiers from Colorado, as did Colonel Irving Hale's troops who saw action in the Philippines.

BLACK BLIZZARDS

Although Colorado had suffered devastating droughts in the late 1800s, the dry years from 1933 to 1938 were the most menacing period ever faced by Eastern Plains farmers. Towering dust storms—"black blizzards"—and hurricanes of sand engulfed towns and swept the land, wiping away fertile top soil and ultimately farmers' livelihoods. So powerful were the tempests that day turned into night and residents switched on the house lights in mid-afternoon. Even ocean-going freighters plying the Atlantic reported fine dust descending upon their decks, testifying to the wide-ranging extent of the natural disaster.

Unable to plant, let alone reap any rewards from their acreage, farmers abandoned the Great Plains. Colorado lost some 15 percent of it farmers and, in some areas, such as the southeastern counties of Baca, Bent and Prowers, the foreclosure rate topped 40 percent. The Eastern Plains had indeed become the "Great American Desert." Primary blame for the environmental holocaust lay with the weather pattern of the "Dirty Thirties." Cold continental air masses shifted, causing moisture-laden tropical air from the Gulf of Mexico to veer east of the Mississippi River leaving the plains desiccated. Others postulated that the calamity stemmed from sun spots and over-active cosmic rays.

Poor rainfall was only part of the cause for the "Dust Bowl" years. For too long farmers relied on agricultural practices better suited to wetter climates and, in the end, they exhausted the sparse resources of the arid plains. The collapse of the soil re-focused efforts to introduce more drought-resistant crops and employ wiser soil management techniques.

Photo: Dust Storm over Burlington, 1934; CHS F-20732.

Top: Founded by Otto Mears in the late 1880s, the Rio Grande Southern Railroad linked 162 miles of track across the southern San Juan Mountains. Mining camps and supply towns were its stops: Ridgeway, Placerville, Telluride, Ophir, Rico, Dolores, Mancos and Durango. When silver prices plummeted with the panic of 1893, the line staggered into financial failure and numerous receiverships.

Nonetheless, the "Southern" survived; it had few rivals for delivering mail, goods and passengers to the struggling San Juan communities. By the 1930s, however, good vehicle roads were encroaching upon the railroad's route and the train's own roadbeds and track were in pitiful condition. The Southern was essentially unable to support heavy rolling stock, and it looked like the "end of the line" for the railroad.

Forest White, superintendent for the Rio Grande Southern, thought differently. With scant financial resources and in dire need of light-weight rolling stock that could maneuver his roadbeds, White dreamed up the "railroad bus." Patched together from a vintage Buick welded to an old railcar, gasoline—not steam—powered the odd-looking contraption. On its maiden run in June, 1931, onlookers were amazed by the ease with which it crested 10,222-foot Lizard Head Pass. Soon, it was dubbed the "Galloping Goose;" passengers thought the rocking ride seemed akin to a fast waddle down the tracks.

Service and speed were decidedly better than lumbering locomotives, and within two years another six "geese" flocked into service. Eventually, three of the brood were converted into excursion cars for sightseers. A one-day roundtrip through the scenic San Juans—"snow-capped 14,000-foot peaks, dashing trout streams, wild flower paradise, historic gold and silver mines"—cost less than $5. Sadly, though, the little buses couldn't outrun the advances of improved motor highways. In 1952, the bulk of the Rio Grande Southern Railroad was sold for scrap. Two "geese" survived, and now nest comfortably as historic monuments in Dolores and Telluride.

Galloping Goose; CHS F-35241, Rio Grande Southern.

America the Beautiful

Colorado has always been associated with the abundant blessings Mother Nature. A year before the "Pikes Peak or Bust Gold Rush," Julia Anna Holmes ascended the mastiff which Zebulon Pike never conquered. She wrote, "In all probability I am the first women who has stood upon the summit of this majestic mountain and gazed upon the wondrous scene."

Other adventurers followed Holmes' example, exploring Colorado's virgin peaks and secret valleys. Those who couldn't come relied on the reports of others. Writer Bayard Taylor published accounts of his 1866 Rocky Mountain tour as *Colorado: A Summer Trip*. It captivated readers. So too did the prose of British traveler Isabella Bird. She arrived in 1873, quickly succumbing to the romantic magnificence of the "storm-rent sentinel" called Longs Peak. In short order, the territory's scenic assets became as well known as its minerals.

Still, Colorado was fast losing it frontier image. Settlement was expanding as mining camps dug deeper into the mountains and water projects unleashed the agricultural potential of plains and plateaus. A few far-sighted people feared the lost of the state's splendor—the victim of plows, pick axes and over-popularity.

Already, the fabulous cliff dwellings of Mesa Verde were under siege from unscrupulous pot hunters. For nearly a decade, Virginia McClurg, a journalist turned lobbyist, harangued Congress for legislation to protect the archaeological wonder. It came in 1906, when the area became a national park.

Enos Mills felt that the glacier-scoured mountains outside Estes Park should also be protected as a national treasure. Congress and President Woodrow Wilson finally agreed with the tireless advocate of Colorado's natural grandeur, creating Rocky Mountain National Park in 1915. The spectacular terrain of snow-capped peaks and montane valley became Colorado's premier nature destination, a testament to the West's beauty for all the nation to enjoy.

Photo opposite: Pikes Peak; CHS F-3837.

MOUNT OF THE HOLY CROSS

Beginning in 1873, William Henry Jackson spent three years exploring Colorado as the chief photographer for the Hayden Survey, which was charged with mapping the central Rocky Mountains. The images that "the photographer of the West" produced became world famous, none more so than that of the *Mount of the Holy Cross.*

The existence of the famed peak—incised with a giant snow-filled cross—was common knowledge in Colorado, though few residents had ever actually seen the phenomenon. Jackson spotted the principal mastiff of the Sawatch Range from atop Grays Peak during late August of 1873. He knew the shot would be good publicity for his team, and he had promised his fiancée a photograph of the enigmatic mountain.

On August 24, the group pressed their mules up the rocky slopes of a nearby mountain. When the pack animals, laden with hundreds of pounds of equipment, could go no farther, Jackson and two assistants completed the ascent with the heavy cameras, only to have swirling fog engulf them. Without blankets or food the men spent a cold night on their vantage point.

The next morning, Jackson took eight photographs of the 14,005-foot peak, images that would both declare Colorado's scenic beauty and sanctify it with mystical significance. It is said that the first picture he took became the most widely reproduced and circulated photo of the 19th century.

Photo: Mount of the Holy Cross; CHS F-2399 Jackson Collection.

Bottom: In 1873, intrepid British traveler and celebrated writer Isabella Bird stopped in the Rocky Mountains during an 18-month, around-the-world tour. While staying at Estes Park, she met "Mountain Jim" Nugent, a hard-drinking, granite-tough Irishman. She described him as a "man about forty-five, and must have been strikingly handsome. He has large grey-blue eyes, deeply set, with well-marked eyebrows, and a handsome aquiline nose. One eye was entirely gone, and the loss made one side of the face repulsive, while the other might have been modeled in marble." Bird convinced Mountain Jim to guide her up Longs Peak. She was 42, in good health, and possessed considerable spunk. Mountain Jim agreed, and during the fine weather of late autumn they set out with two companions. They spent the first night camped at the base of Longs Peak, and the next morning began their trek to the summit. During the climb, Mountain Jim roped Bird to him to prevent her slipping away on the loose rock. She later reported that he literally dragged her to the top of the peak. Bird loved the journey, however, which placed her "on one of the mightiest of the vertebrae of the backbone" of North America. Her stories of adventure in the West were later published in 1879 as *A Lady's Life in the Rocky Mountains*.
Isabella Bird; CHS F-7084.

Top: Named for Major Stephen Long, Longs Peak was never actually ascended by the famous explorer. At 14,255 feet, there are 14 higher Colorado mountains, but the setting of Longs Peak amidst the Front Range is magnificent, easily explaining why adventurers were drawn to the mountain. William Byers, editor of the *Rocky Mountain News*, came in 1864 to climb the peak. He failed to reach the mount's summit but wrote glowing reports of the spectacular scenery, which encouraged others to visit.
Longs Peak Panorama; CHS F-44870.

AMERICA THE BEAUTIFUL

On July 22, 1893, Katharine Lee Bates, a Massachusetts English teacher, ascended Pikes Peak. She descended with two lines of poetry: *"Oh beautiful for spacious skies, For amber waves of grain."* It's a Colorado souvenir the entire nation now enjoys.

Born in 1859, Bates' love for words urged her into an English degree at Wellesley College. Her other love, travel, brought her to Colorado Springs. She joined other professors, including future president Woodrow Wilson, to teach the summer quarter at Colorado College. Bates and several companions celebrated session's end with an expedition up Pikes Peak.

The visit lasted only a moment. Two of the party sickened with the altitude; the driver insisted they descend. Bates later wrote, "The Peak remains in memory hardly more than one ecstatic gaze." That night, she expanded her couplet:

> *For purple mountain majesties*
> *Above the fruited plain!*
> *America! America!*

> *God shed His grace on thee*
> *And crown thy good with*
> *brotherhood*
> *From sea to shining sea!*

On July 4, 1895, her lines appeared in *The Congregationalist* magazine. On the fifth, Bates was a celebrity. Sixty composers volunteered tunes to match her meter. Bates dutifully sang out each, but none quite fit. Searching hymnals she discovered S. A. Ward's *O Mother Dear, Jerusalem*. It harmonized perfectly. Together, words and melody expressed the lofty sentiments of a proud nation.

Photos: Pikes Peak; CHS F-6389. Pikes Peak Halfway House; CHS.

Bottom: Burros were the preferred pack animals for prospectors and in this case, for railroad builders too. This mother and baby, straddling the ratchet-type tracks of the cog railway, proclaim their contribution to Colorado's railroad legacy: "We Helped Build Pikes Peak R.R." Construction on the Manitou and Pikes Peak Railway began on September 25, 1889, and was complet-

ed 13 months later. The Highlands Christian Church choir of Denver were the first to ascend Pikes Peak by rail on June 30, 1891.
Burros; CHS Neg. # 3872 Jackson Collection.

Top: When comfort-minded Zalmon Simmons, of Simmons Mattress fame and fortune, scaled Pikes Peak atop a mule in the late 1800s, he proclaimed the scenery stunning but the journey too

strenuous. He remedied the situation by installing a Swiss-style cog railway to negotiate the perilous grades that sometimes reached 25 percent en route to the top. Gears beneath the engine zippered their way up a set of teeth set between the rails that stretched for nearly nine miles past vistas with evocative names such as "Son-of-a-Gun Hill" and "Hell Gate." In 1925, mining millionaire Spencer Penrose purchased the railroad, adding it to his Colorado Springs commercial interests such as the Broadmoor Hotel. He invested heavily in modernizing the railway, equipping it with new gasoline-powered engines, a much-appreciated improvement over the cinder- and smoke-spewing coal-fired steam locomotives.
Cog Railway; CHS Buckwalter Book I, #52.

GENERAL PALMER

Colorado Springs owes its existence to a Civil War veteran, General William Jackson Palmer. After the war, Palmer traveled west as a surveyor for the Kansas Pacific Railroad. He favored the idea of a route up the Arkansas River to the Front Range and from there, north to Denver. Produce from the Arkansas Valley and Pueblo's industrial output would fill the boxcars. His bosses, however, chose a more direct line across the northern plains.

Palmer didn't forsake his plan; launching in 1871 the Denver and Rio Grande Railroad. This man of vision concurrently formed the Colorado Springs Company to create a resort enclave with Pikes Peak as the postcard backdrop. Within a year, tracks ran 76 miles south from Denver to the newly formed town. Palmer envisioned Colorado Springs as a health-inducing retreat for socialites, and soon the town became the "Newport of the Rockies."

After his wife's death, Palmer expanded his Victorian-style Glen Eyrie estate—nestled in the Garden of the Gods—into a baronial castle.

Photos: Palmer; CHS F-3338. Glen Eyrie; CHS. William Jackson and Family; F-31371.

BROADMOOR

Early in Colorado Springs' history, a *bon vivant* German nobleman, Count James Graf von Pourtales, often graced the drawing rooms of the city's élite.

The Count was an aspiring real estate mogul occupying his time with the construction of a posh residential area on a former dairy farm: Broadmoor. Water for the homes would come from a new reservoir, created by an earthen dam. Alas, townsfolk feared for the dike's integrity, and as an act of panache, Pourtales borrowed $250,000 from New York friends to encase the dam in concrete and erect the swank Broadmoor Casino in its foreground. It would be a "Palace of Pleasure" and one of the few places in Colorado Springs where gentlemen could drink and gamble.

The massive construction effort left Pourtales virtually penniless; his only income from the venture was liquor sales. To restore his fortune, he invested in promising Cripple Creek mining claims. Nonetheless, a new fortune evaded the Count. In 1895, the Broadmoor Casino burned.

Colorado Springs tycoon Spencer Penrose purchased the property in 1916, pumping nearly $3 million into an extensive reconstruction. The result was the new Broadmoor Hotel. Its luxury immediately established the complex as Colorado's pre-eminent retreat, a reputation still enjoyed by the resort.

Photos: Broadmoor Casino; CHS F-7074. Count Pourtales; CHS F-7077.

Top: Many early immigrants to Colorado were health-seekers. The territory's clear, dry mountain air and invigorating climate was seen as a cure-all for a range of maladies, in particularly diseases of the lungs. It is telling that 25 percent of recorded deaths in Denver at the turn of the century resulted from tuberculosis.

Manitou Springs, ensconced on the mild-weather lee side of Pikes Peak, attracted many sufferers, who relished the miraculous mineral springs. Physicians of the day proclaimed the waters a tonic to stimulate the blood and ease the digestive system.
Manitou Springs Spa; CHS WHJ Cities Notebook 2245.

Bottom: On Colorado's Western Slope, Glenwood Springs commercially tapped their famous mineral waters in 1893. The Italianate-styled Hotel Colorado featured an expansive swimming pool, 110 feet wide by 640 feet long, which easily accommodated hundreds of vacationers seeking a relaxing retreat from Victorian-era stress.
Glenwood Springs Girl; CHS F-11287 Buckwalter Notebook.

Bottom: Bucolically genteel pastimes occupied Victorian-era residents of the "Centennial State." A favorable climate encouraged outdoor excursions to dawdle amidst Mother Nature's sylvan wonders. These ladies found an ideal spot along Denver's South Platte River to wile away a few hours while lazily fishing with twig poles.
Women Fishing South Platte; CHS W-71 Lillybridge Collection.

Top: Colorado's economic crisis of the 1890s tempted many communities to court tourism as a financial patron. At Leadville in 1896, more than 200 workers spent two months erecting a mock-Norman castle from ice blocks. The completed "Ice Palace," with eight-foot thick walls, covered five acres and stood from January to March before it finally began to melt. Thousands of visitors marveled at its fairytale grandeur, its carnival exhibits and its amusements, such as ice skating and ballroom dancing.
Leadville Ice Palace; CHS F-6637.

Opposite: To protect Colorado's fragile Ancestral Puebloan cliff dwellings, the U.S. Congress created 82-square-mile Mesa Verde National Park in 1906, the first park dedicated to preserving the works of humankind. Dr. Jesse Walter Fewkes was an archaeologist with the Smithsonian Institute. While conducting digs at Mesa Verde in 1915, he initiated "campfire programs," which would become one of the national park system's most popular guest activities.
Dr. Fewkes and Cliff Palace; CHS F-38920.

Bottom: In a conundrum that still baffles scientists, the Ancestral Puebloan cliff dwellings at Mesa Verde were mysteriously forsaken during the 13th century. The Utes came to the area in the 1500s, found the ruins too haunting and kept to the river valleys. Spanish missionary Juan Maria Rivera journeyed here in 1765 to trade with the Utes and no doubt came upon the site. Survey parties mapped the canyonlands in the late 1800s, and William Henry Jackson took pictures of "Two Story Cliff House" in 1874.
Mesa Verde; CHS F-40531.

Top: It wasn't until 1888, when ranchers Richard Wetherill and Charlie Mason came upon the "Cliff Palace," that Mesa Verde's true wonders came to light. One cold December day, the cowboys paused while searching for strays on a slickrock overhang on Chapin Mesa and spied the massive structure with more than 200 rooms. The Wetherills (part of the family seen here at a Ute wedding) collected a number of artifacts, which were later sold and exhibited. Soon, archaeologists and souvenir-hunters were combing the area, threatening to wipe clean any lasting record of the Ancestral Puebloans.
Weatherill with Utes; CHS F-36408.

F.O. Stanley opened the posh Stanley Hotel
outside Estes Park in 1909.

LORD DUNRAVEN

Irish aristocrat Lord Dunraven came to Estes Park in the 1870s. He liked the region so much that he acquired 15,000 acres for his sole noble pleasure. Being a foreigner, and therefore restricted from homesteading, didn't dissuade him. He skirted the law, having others (not always alive) front for him on 160-acre parcels, which were then transferred to his Britain-based "English Company." In time, legitimate homesteaders discovered his scheme and forced him into leasing arrangements. Dunraven eventually grew tired of the squabbles, selling most of his holdings to a partnership headed by F.O. Stanley.

Lord Dunraven; CHS.

ENOS MILLS

While the efforts of many people contributed to the formation of Rocky Mountain National Park, Enos Mills is remembered as its most ardent supporter.

Mills first came to the area in 1884 at the age of 14. By 1890, he had claimed a homestead at the foot of Longs Peak. From his tiny cabin, he supported himself as a professional guide and naturalist. In 1902, he purchased the Longs Peak Inn where guests availed themselves of his expert mountaineering services.

territory a "wildlife preserve," advocating that it should include more than 1,000 square miles and extend from Estes Park to Colorado Springs.

President Theodore Roosevelt backed Mills and commissioned him to undertake cross-country lectures to promote the land's preservation. Mills proved to be an excellent speaker and an effective naturalist writer, penning articles for the *Saturday Evening Post, Harper's* and *Atlantic*, in addition to several books. The campaign finally paid off in 1915 when Congress and President Woodrow Wilson created Rocky Mountain National Park, the nation's tenth national park. It was less than half the size originally proposed by Mills. But at least it now become a sanctuary for future generations, a place to "put one in tune with the Infinite," as Mills wrote.

In time, Mills and other long-time residents of the region could see the toll that development was taking on the glacier moraines and alpine highlands they loved. Although the area was now largely contained within the Medicine Bow Forest Reserve, the designation did little to secure the fragile environment. Mills wholeheartedly endorsed suggestions to make the

Photos: Enos Mills; CHS F-43672, Enos and his dog "Scotch." Tree; CHS, photo of windblown tree perhaps taken by Mills.

Top: Freelan Oscar Stanley, a wealthy inventor, came to Colorado to ease his tuberculosis. The clear alpine air inspired him and soon he envisioned Estes Park as the ideal place for overworked Victorian socialites. In 1909, he opened the posh Stanley Hotel, ferrying guests to the mountain retreat from the railway station at Lyons via handsome Stanley Steamer Mountain Wagons.
Stanley Steamer in Estes Park; CHS F-21356.

Bottom: In 1929, the construction of Trail Ridge Road through Rocky Mountain National Park was initiated, taking four years to complete. Road crews were restricted to working only during the summer due to the high altitude and months of snow. In the end, the route traversed some 10 miles of alpine terrain, half of which higher than 12,000 feet above sea level, making it the highest paved automobile road in the United States. The Alpine Visitor Center at the crest of Fall River Pass provided a welcome rest stop and a good place to stretch road-weary legs with brisk hikes through the tundra.
Trail Ridge Road Alpine Visitor Center; CHS F-34725.

Top: Rocky Mountain National Park had few visitor services when it opened in 1915 and for a time, the Rocky Mountain Parks Transportation Company enjoyed exclusive rights to provide public transportation in the park. Fall River Road was already under construction but it would take convict crews until 1920 to cleave the narrow, twisting route into the park's high-altitude tundra. With the opening of the route, scenic excursions via private car became the pre-eminent way to experience Rocky Mountain National Park. More than 250,000 people came to the park during 1920, all seeking a natural escape from civilization. *Rocky Mountain Parks Transportation; CHS.*

Opposite: The introduction of domesticated sheep and their diseases, and the encroachment of humans nearly decimated the bighorn sheep population in Rocky Mountain National Park. Admired for their sure-footedness, only males display the distinctive curved horns. The agile creature of per- ilous escarpments was declared the Colorado state animal in 1961.
Sheep Head; CHS 106 Detroit Publishing.

Bottom: Grand Lake, located on the western side of Rocky Mountain National Park, is the largest natural body of water in Colorado. Utes and Arapahos both favored the area and once fought a bloody battle on its shores. The Utes, fearing for the safety of their women and children, placed them on a raft and set it adrift on the lake. However, a tremendous storm rose up, capsizing the raft and drowning its occupants.

The Utes believe that the steamy vapors rising from the lake on cool mornings are the souls of their departed ancestors, hence their name for the waters, "Spirit Lake." Miners dug for ore in the late 1800s, but the area's true treasure became the lake itself. Many early Coloradans spent summer vacations by the lake, braving its bracing waters and fishing for salmon and trout.
Grand Lake; CHS F-22864 McClure Boxed Collection.

Opposite: Rising to 13,514 feet, Ypsilon Mountain in Rocky Mountain National Park is named for the peaks distinctive Y-shaped snow-field, which crosses its stony east face. *Ypsilon* is the word for the letter "Y" in Greek. This German spelling notes the predominance of early European mountaineers.
Mt. Ypsilon; CHS Rocky Mountain Photo Co., Louis Holland.

Bottom: Situated on the Continental Divide in Rocky Mountain National Park, Hallett Peak (12,713 feet) was named for the founder of the Rocky Mountain Club. The 415-square-mile park holds more than 100 mountains over 11,000 feet and shelters a tundra environment known for ferocious winters and short summers.
Hallett Peak; CHS Louis Holland.

Top: Adventurist Agnes Vaille, seen here with two members of the Colorado Mountain Club atop 13,223-foot Mount Audubon, was one of Colorado's most intrepid climbers. She made the first recorded winter ascent of 13,294-foot James Peak on the Continental Divide. Known as a "strong, husky woman, just crazy about climbing," Vaille died of hypothermia during a descent of the east face of Longs Peak on January 12, 1925.
Agnes Vaille; CHS F-44870.

Opposite: The mining depression of the 1890s forced many railroads to hitch their cars to new prospects. Tourist excursion trains became popular, and railroads developed special rates and packages for visitors who were eager to see Colorado's high country. Brochures extolled the virtues of the state's scenic superlatives and celebrities such as Jack Fox, alias "Buster Brown," hopped aboard to promote the tourism potential of railroad routes, and to advertise popular Buster Brown shoes.
Buster Brown and Train; CHS I#34 Colorado Midland.

Bottom: Gathering wildflowers in the Rocky Mountain's alpine regions became a much-loved pastime for turn-of-the-century tourists. Columbines were greatly treasured as keepsakes of a memorable outing into the high country. However, rampant collection of the showy buds prevented them from seeding, nearly decimating the bloom that would later become the Colorado state flower. In 1925, law was enacted to protect the flower in its natural habitat.
Columbine Pickers; CHS F-31766 Colorado Midland.

Top: Right from the beginning, the Colorado Midland became a favorite with train excursionists. An engineering marvel, the train huffed and puffed west out of Colorado Springs to the eastern footings of the breathtaking Sawatch Range, then north along the upper reaches of the Arkansas River to Leadville. Trains often stopped at Sphinx Rock north of Buena Vista, allowing tourists to stretch their legs and pose for photos.
Tourist Train Sphinx Rock; CHS I#80 Colorado Midland.

Opposite: Under the guidance of poet, lecturer and lobbyist Virginia McClurg, the Colorado Cliff Dwelling Association sponsored the protection of Mesa Verde. On occasion, the group also mounted theater productions such as the *Pageant of the marriage of the Dawn and the Moon* by McClurg, within the sacred confines of the mysterious Ancestral Puebloans. *CHS.*

Bottom: Miner turned naturalist Edwin Carter came to Colorado in the height of the "Pikes Peak or Bust Gold Rush." He assembled an impressive array of mounted Colorado fauna. Denver officials expressed interest in acquiring his taxidermic arts and Carter agreed to part with his life's work if a fireproof building were erected to house it. By 1908, the Denver Museum of Natural History housed Carter's collection.
Mr. Carter and Wolf; CHS Buckwalter Collection.

Top: Car camping became a cost-effective way for many travelers to see the U.S.A. Responding to the trend of "gypsy motorists" in 1915, Denver purchased Overland Park (along the South Platte River), making it one of the country's first municipal campgrounds. Within a decade, Colorado had over 250 auto camps, temporarily housing more than 500,000 campers a year.
Car Camping; CHS F-33994 Colorado Hwy. Dept. Boxed Collection.

Rocky Mountain High

World War II was a tonic to Colorado, boosting an impressive economic revival as the state shed the burden of the Great Depression. It also changed the "Centennial State" forever. The many needs of the war machine matched well with Colorado's natural resources. A personal price was exacted, beyond the frustration of ration books and the dearth of consumer goods. An eighth of the population, more than 130,000 citizens, enlisted or were drafted into military service. Some 2,700 never saw their home again.

Military mobilization was of the highest order for the nation and Colorado figured prominently in the plans of Pentagon strategists. The state's annual military payroll ballooned to nearly $152 million by 1944, up from $3 million in 1940. The effects could be seen all along the Front Range.

Denver saw the Army Air Corp move into Lowry Field. Buckley Field opened farther east of Denver and, on the west side of town, the Denver Ordinance Plant employed 20,000—half of which were women—to churn out .30-caliber ammunition. Ship hulls for escort vehicles such as the *U.S.S. Mountain Maiden* were also launched at Denver factories. In 1942, the Rocky Mountain Arsenal opened to produce chemical weapons.

Colorado Springs housed Peterson Field in addition to the state's largest military installation, Fort Carson. More than 150,000 troops of the 89th, 71st and 104th divisions were trained here for active duty in Europe. The military brass would remember Colorado Springs in the 1950s, selecting it as the site for the ultra-secretive North American Air Defense Command (NORAD) and the prestigious Air Force Academy.

Colorado's mountains weren't spared the army's aim either. Camp Hale, located outside Leadville, opened in 1942, becoming home to 15,000 men. The high-altitude environment was ideal for training in extreme winter conditions, excellent preparation for the 10th Mountain Division who would see action in the Italian Alps.

At the government's insistence, mining turned away from

gold and silver to coal for power plants, and molybdenum, tungsten and vanadium for steel production. With the coming of the Cold War, a uranium boom erupted on the Uncompahgre Plateau as "weekend prospectors" searched for the atomic weapon fuel. Oil production, a nascent industry in Colorado, gushed as pump-jacks nodded in the prairies. From 1940 to the mid-1950s, annual oil output leaped from less than 2 million barrels to nearly 60 million barrels of "black gold."

With Colorado's economic rise new residents arrived, many of them military retirees. Housing development along the Front Range became an industry of its own. By 1950, Denver and its adjacent counties accounted for more than 40 percent of the state's overall population.

The newcomers relished the climate and scenery, setting out to see the sights and experience its pleasures. The old mineral belt that sliced across the state from the Front Range to the San Juans would be transformed into the "ski belt," as onetime mining enclaves reinvented themselves into alpine attractions. What was once a sleepy state with a cowtown capital was now the darling of the New West.

Photo Top: Rocky Mountain Clipper; CHS Denver Municipal Airport, 1937 Jean Nelson.

Top: From 1942 until 1944, a prestigious U.S. Army unit—the 10th Mountain Division—trained for winter maneuvers in the Pando Valley situated in the Holy Cross National Forest between Leadville and Minturn. Comprised of 15,000 men from around the country, they would serve out their military duty in extreme cold and high altitude, usually on skis. Camp Hale became their home. Here, they honed their skiing skills and perfected the basics of winter survival and fighting in the snow. Training sessions ended with strenuous week-long bivouacs at Homestead Peak.
Camp Hale Overview; CHS.

Bottom: When the 10th Mountain Division soldiers weren't on clean-up duty, the men carried 90-pound rucksacks on their backs as they trekked up then skied down the nearby slopes of Cooper Hill. They developed special boots that could be used on both skis and snowshoes as well as for hiking and climbing. Soldiers even had a way to attach packs to their skis in case they needed a toboggan.
Clean-up Crew; CHS.

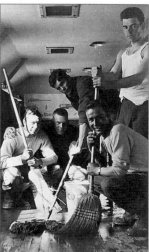

Skiers 10th Mountain Division; CHS F-10569.

Top: Troops of the 92nd Chemical Company conducted maneuvers to perfect the use of gas masks while wearing bulky winter clothing. Reports indicate difficulty manipulating the gear while wearing mittens. The 10th Mountain Division solved hundreds of small and large problems during their alpine training. In 1945, the troops saw action in the Appenine Mountains of northern Italy, successfully putting their Colorado lessons to the test against German strongholds.
Camp Hale Skiers; CHS "Sweetbriar" Exercise.

Bottom: Conducting a precision "About Face" while wearing long skis required practice, though many of the soldiers of the 10th Mountain Division were already skilled alpine skiers. After the war, many 10th Mountain Division veterans chose to return to the bracing mountains of the "Centennial State." Understandably, with their consummate skiing abilities, they fostered the emerging Colorado ski industry serving roles from instructors to resort developers.

AMACHE

Two months after the Japanese surprise attack on Pearl Harbor in December 1941, President Franklin D. Roosevelt signed Executive Order 9066. The mandate called for the relocation of 110,000 Japanese-Americans from California, Arizona, Oregon and Washington.

Many Japanese-Americans vacated the deportation zone voluntarily. Denver's modest-sized Japanese community grew as West Coast family and friends became new residents of the "Mile High City." For those who lacked the financial means to relocate, 10 detention camps were established in the U.S. interior to house them. One of those settlements was Amache, outside the town of Granada on Colorado's southeastern plains. By October 1942, the wooden-barrack enclave surrounded by stout wire fence was home to 7,576 Japanese-Americans.

Of the total population, some two-thirds held U.S. citizenship. Many of the younger men enlisted in the U.S. military to serve alongside their fellow Americans to defeat the Japanese Imperial forces.

Those who stayed behind contributed to the Arkansas Valley's agricultural industry, plowing fields and harvesting sugar beets, melons and potatoes. The barren prairie they called home quickly became a well-organized and productive community with its own internal government, schools for the youngsters and even a local newspaper.

Amache's brief blossoming on the Great Plains withered in July 1945, when the camp was closed. While most of the internees returned to their former homes, more than 2,000 chose to stay in Colorado and begin a new life.

Photo: Amache; CHS F-32705.

Top: Colorado's wide-open spaces and geographic isolation from both the Atlantic and Pacific coasts were ideal training-ground criteria for military planners gearing up the war effort. Denver alone soon housed thousands of new recruits, especially at Lowry Field, founded in 1924 as the headquarters of the 120th Observation Squadron.

Functioning primarily as an armament and military photography school, World War II bolstered its cadet roster considerably. By 1941, Lowry Field received more than a 1,000 students a week. Instructors and pupils coped with 18-hour school days, which were run on two shifts. With the beginning of 1942, the War Department increased Lowry Field's training requirements to 55,000 men annually.

Course study for enlistees of the 36th and 37th Bombardment Squadrons lasted 16 weeks. Three classes graduated between July of 1940 and March of 1941, receiving commissions as Second Lieutenants. They would become a core group of trainers for instructing more than 15,000 bombardiers during World War II. Recruits, such as these men shown here shouldering 100-pound dummy bombs, practiced the teamwork required to effectively flight-ready a B-18A.

At the war's end, Lowry Field served as a separation center for the Army Air Forces, discharging some 300 men a day. In 1947, the Air Force was separated from the Army, creating the United States Air Force and the need for a dedicated academy for officer training. Lowry Air Force Base would temporarily house that institution until the completion of the Air Force Academy outside Colorado Springs. *Lowry Field; CHS.*

Top: Having survived a near bankruptcy and reorganization in the 1930s, Pueblo's Colorado Fuel and Iron (CF&I) found itself ignited in the 1940s by the voracious steel needs of the war effort. In 1940, the company received its first war production order for 5,000 forgings of 155-millimeter shells. A year later, the company committed to making additional casings, in all forming more than three million projectiles over the next three years.
CF&I Pueblo; CHS F-44019.

Bottom: To create the 155 mm shells, 30-foot steel billets from rolling mills were heated to 2,250 degrees Fahrenheit, then forged into shape and lathed into projectile form. The finished shells were sent to ordinance plants for production of the actual artillery rounds. Intense heat and noise during the shell's manufacturing meant that workers could labor for only 45 minutes at time, recuperating for the remainder of the hour before resuming their tasks. In 1944, CF&I's 500 workers set a world production record: 27,844 shell casings in six days.
CF&I Workers; CHS F-2074.

demand for their produce. *Tractor in Field; CHS E.K. Edwards Collection.*

Top: During the 1930s' depression years and for some time afterward, Colorado agricultural output remained low. Farm production stayed low to counterbalance sagging prices for produce and grain. That changed with the coming of the war. The demand for food supplies created a bonanza: ample returns for abundant crops. Colorado land value jumped as acreage that had lain fallow for years was now plowed for fields of corn, wheat and feed grains for cattle. *Truck in Field; CHS E.K. Edwards Collection.*

Bottom: Colorado's agricultural boom continued throughout the 1940s, supplying the war effort and fulfilling the post-war foodstuff needs to aid Europe's reconstruction under the Marshall Plan. Water and soil conservationists feared a return to the perilous agricultural practices that created the "Dust Bowl" days as farmers sowed increasingly extensive tracts of land to meet the

URANIUM: THE ATOMIC BOMB

Colorado's Western Slope became "the land of the weekend prospector" during the late 1940s and early 1950s. The Cold War was in high gear and the U.S. military required uranium to fuel atomic weapon production.

The Atomic Energy Commission encouraged casual prospecting. The U.S. Government Printing Office published a pamphlet for novice miners explaining how to find the yellow carbonite ore. With instructions in one hand, and a Geiger counter in the other, rock hounds roamed the Uncompahgre Plateau looking to strike it rich.

Uranium discoveries did equate to wealth. Colorado produced in excess of $133 million of uranium from 1948 to 1960. Grand Junction became the headquarters for more than 100 uranium companies. Mining towns such as Uravan, Nucla and Naturita mushroomed, as did milling and ore reduction centers such as Durango, Rifle, Gunnison and Cañon City. By the 1960s, the boom was silenced. Government support cratered as operation costs skyrocketed. Public concern also spiked; the nuclear era's long-term hazardous effects were coming to light.

Curiously, increased public pressure followed by government intervention lead to a residual uranium boom. More than $360 million would be expended to seal, relocate, or destroy the toxic residue of uranium's bright day of mining and processing. Not counted in this financial assessment would be the human suffering. Hundreds of Coloradans were unknowingly exposed to radon gas emissions, a natural by-product of uranium. Lung cancer and other ailments would be the price they paid for this Colorado mining explosion.

Photo: Uravan; CHS Denver Post Historical Collection.

Top: The prestigious United States Air Force Academy located north of Colorado Springs was established in 1954, surpassing 580 other proposed sites around the nation. The Academy's mission is to provide instruction and experience so that cadets attain the essential leadership qualities for officer rank in the United States Air Force. Each year, some 12,000 men and women apply for entry into the institution; only 1,400 are accepted. Those lucky few face a rigorous four-year challenge in military studies, academics, athletics and character development, including moral and ethical studies. In the end, cadets possess a firm foundation—mentally, physically and emotionally—in order to graduate with "the right stuff."

Set against the backdrop of the Rampart Range, the multi-spired chapel building is the centerpiece of the 18,000-acre campus. Beneath the 150-foot-high aluminum spires, light streams in on a Protestant chapel with a 46-foot-high crucifix above the altar; a Catholic chapel is bathed in light from an abstract mosaic mural; a Jewish synagogue is focused on the Aaron Kodesh, the Holy Ark sheltering the Scrolls of the Torah; and an all-faiths room is purposely devoid of all religious symbols. All services can be conducted simultaneously.

The Air Force Academy, as seen from this aerial shot, sets against the Rampart Range, foothills to Colorado's central Rocky Mountains.

Chapel Air Force Academy; CHS. Photo page 100-101: Air Force Academy aerial shot; CHS.

Opposite: Ensigns of both the United States and Canada, the two partner nations that operate the impregnable fortress of the North American Aerospace Defense Command (NORAD) stand sentinel before the facility's unassuming entrance. Constructed within a hollowed-out chamber of hard-granite Cheyenne Mountain, the installation south of Colorado Springs was built to withstand nuclear attack. Twenty-five-foot-thick steel doors seal the entrance and the entire command rests on 1,319 half-ton, shock-absorbing springs. Through the portal is a city of 11 steel buildings, including Combat Operations Center, which oversees North America's nuclear arsenal.
NORAD Cave Entrance; CHS.

Bottom: Colorado's continued military presence induced a number of key industrial concerns, which supply various armed forces, to locate facilities near their important clients. The Front Range from Fort Collins to Pueblo became the headquarters for numerous military research and manufacturing installations. Defense giant Martin Marrietta opened the Waterton Plant near Denver to build Titan I missiles, which were transported by the "Guppy," a modified Boeing 377.
Guppy; CHS Stapleton Airport, photo by Gene Elliott.

Top: NORAD's Space Defense Center receives data from a network of space-watching devices. Attendants catalogue all human-made objects circling earth, determining their orbits and calculating future positions. This is essential information to differentiate benign high-altitude objects from potential threats to North America.
NORAD Space Defense Center; CHS F-37,365.

Top: Although 19th-century miners occasionally donned 11-foot-long "Norwegian snowshoes" to traverse the snowy terrain, it wasn't until after World War II that Colorado's skiing industry hit the slopes in full force. Two events put Aspen on the map and lifted the sport's growth. Wealthy Chicago industrialist Walter Paepcke and his wife Elizabeth sponsored the Goethe Bicentennial celebration in 1949, introducing the quaint mining town to hundreds of cultural giants. And in 1950, Aspen hosted the International Federation of Skiing (FIS) World Skiing Championships, confirming the locale as a skier's dream come true.
Aspen Skiers; CHS F-32496.

Bottom: Aspen's Lift No. 1 opened on January 11, 1947 on the west side of Ajax Mountain. It was the longest and fastest chairlift in the world. The 19-year-old daughter of the mayor, Allene Robison, was the first passenger, followed by other dignitaries such as national ski champion Dick Durrance and celebrities such as actor Gary Cooper. Other Lift No. 1 riders have included "Bingo," a St. Bernard belonging to Fred Iselin, a director of Aspen Ski School in the 1950s.
Bingo Rides; Aspen Historical Society #C-1037, Miggs Durrance Photo.

Bottom: Facilities at Colorado's newly developed ski resorts were basic. Single chairs, hung from frighteningly long cables, greeted skiers to Aspen's Lift No. 1. In the late 1940s, the Ski Inn Restaurant at the base of No. 1 served as the much-appreciated warming hut and place for a leisurely bite to eat. Skiers often waited up to an hour for a ride up the lift. The Ski Inn Restaurant, renamed the Skier's Cafe, burned down in 1952, and was replaced by the Skier's Chalet which is still in operation. *Ski Inn Restaurant; Aspen Historical Society #A-1039.*

Top: During the late 1800's, Aspen's prodigious Smuggler Mine produced the world's largest silver nugget, weighing in at 1,840 pounds. In the coming century, skiing would become Aspen's new currency, transforming the sleepy mining community into the darling of the ski industry. Early investors picked up shares of the Aspen Skiing Corp. for 33 cents a share, eventually selling them in 1978 at $45 per share when 20th Century Fox purchased the company. Average prices for homes easily exceed the $1 million mark today, even more for something as historic as the Sardy House pictured here. It is the one-time home of J.W. "Three Finger Jack" Atkinson, an early Aspen entrepreneur involved in freighting and mining. *Sardy House; Aspen Historical Society #A-1041.*

Opposite: Colorado's favorable winter mountain climate of 300 average inches of "champagne powder" and nearly 300 days of sunshine, encouraged many of the state's alpine areas to look at snow enthusiasts for their financial future. Early ski clubs created winter carnivals and, by 1919, members of the Rocky Mountain Ski Club sponsored the state's first National Ski Championships. By 1940, Winter Park, located at the west portal of Moffat Tunnel, was dedicated as Colorado's first major ski area. Aspen would define the concept of a world-class ski resort, signaling the development of others such as Breckenridge, Vail, Crested Butte, Telluride and Steamboat Springs.
Ski Tracks; CHS F-32157.

Bottom: From the very beginning, Aspen and other resorts attracted skiing's top talent. Olympic racers John Litchfield and Percy Rideout helped establish the Aspen Ski School. Steve Knowlton, a national skiing champion and Olympian, opened Aspen's first nightclub, the Golden Horn. Winner of 17 national championships, Dick Durrance, served as the general manager of the Aspen Skiing Corp. Pictured here is Peter Siebert, veteran of the 10th Mountain Division and later co-founder of Vail.
Peter Siebert, Aspen Ski School; CHS F-31948.

Top: St. Mary's Glacier, near Idaho Springs, had a distinct advantage over Colorado's emerging winter downhill playgrounds: as a glacier it sports snow year-round. Adventurous skiers could test their mettle against a variety of challengers, even motorcyclists.
Skier with Motorcyclists; CHS F-13335 - St. Mary's Glacier.

THE EISENHOWER YEARS

The eight years of the Eisenhower presidency (1953-1961) were good to Colorado. The president and first lady were frequent visitors to the "Centennial State" and the media who followed them cast an alluring spotlight on its natural splendor.

The Eisenhowers were long acquainted with Colorado. Mamie Geneva Doud Eisenhower could trace her Colorado connection to age six when her family moved from Cedar Rapids, Iowa, to Pueblo, Colorado. The family subsequently resided in Colorado Springs and later, in Denver at 750 Lafayette Street.

For Dwight and Mamie the house bore fond memories; they were married here on July 1, 1916. On that same day "Ike" became not only a husband; he also received his first army promotion, receiving the insignia of a first lieutenant. It would be just one of many achievements as

THE EISENHOWER YEARS

viewed as a gracious hostess and first lady. She regularly placed in the top ten on the Gallup Poll's list of most admired women. The couple's visits to Colorado portrayed a life of comfort and ease. Here, they escaped the rigors of public life, flying in on the presidential plane, *Columbine*, named after Colorado's state flower. While staying in the "Centennial State" they reveled in simple pleasures such as playing cards, attending quiet social events, or exploring the mountain parks on fishing trips.

Ike's favorite fishing stream was on the Aksel Nielsen Byers Peak ranch near Fraser and the family loved to entertain at the Ship Tavern Restaurant in the Brown Palace Hotel, where the couple frequently stayed. The Browns' suite number 825 was their address and shared with offices at Lowry Air Force Base the moniker of the "Summer White House." People from around the world who saw pictures and read reports of the "presidential playground" would now include Colorado in their future vacation plans.

the career military man rose through the ranks to become the Supreme Commander of Allied Expeditionary Forces during World War II, and ultimately, the 34th president of the United States.

Ike and Mamie were a popular first family, the president enjoying a respected reputation as a competent commander-in-chief, and Mamie

Photos: Ike Flag; CHS F-38028, photo by David Mathias. Ike and Mamie; CHS Denver Post Historical Collection, photo by Dean Conger. Ike with Beet; CHS Denver Post Historical Collection, photo by Dean Conger.

Organized into the American Football League in 1959, the Denver Broncos lost all their pre-season games in 1960. However, the Broncos were the victors in history's first AFL game, beating the Boston Patriots 13-10. Frank Tripucka, #18, was the Bronco's quarterback from 1960-63. Professional sports would become one of Colorado's growth industries and an integral part of Denver's civic pride and that of the state as a whole. Like all of the "Centennial State's" previous brushes with fame and fortune, this one also promised its share of booms and busts.
Denver Broncos; CHS F-38865, Denver Post photo.

About the Authors

Dan Klinglesmith

Patrick Soran

Writer and photographer Dan Klinglesmith can trace his Colorado roots back four generations. His great-great grandparents, John and Martha Barrow, came to the "Centennial State" in 1888, settling in Crested Butte. The mining camp was too rowdy a place to raise children so they moved to Hotchkiss, homesteading a few acres outside town on what is still called Barrow Mesa. Born on the Western Slope at Grand Junction, Dan fondly remembers summers spent horseback riding amidst the buttes and valleys that were first settled by his family.

Growing up on the state's Front Range gave Dan a taste of big-city life, and he still calls Denver home. For the last decade, however, the world has become his backyard. Working as a freelance travel writer and photographer, Dan has crisscrossed the globe, penning articles for a wide variety of magazines and newspapers.

Nevertheless, he admits there's no place like home. "Colorado has it all," contends Dan. "It's a state marked with incredible natural beauty, fascinating history and diversions to occupy a lifetime." He adds, "there's no greater joy than writing about the place you love."

Raised and educated in Denver's Capitol Hill, Patrick Soran lives in the very home in which he was born. The house was purchased by his grandparents in 1936 and has served as hearth and home to three generations. Needless to say, Patrick is an enthusiastic advocate of Denver; he loves to pedal its bicycle paths, chat with friends in its urbane coffee shops, walk its tree-lined avenues and, of course, spend autumn Sundays cheering (and crying!) for the Denver Broncos.

Trained as an architect, Patrick designed luxury homes and hotel interiors for 15 years before trading T-square and triangle for computer and camera in 1990. Now he explores the world writing articles about travel, design and personalities for newspapers and magazines across the country.

Patrick is immensely proud to write about his home state. He believes Colorado has terrific wilderness and wildlife experiences, edge-of-the-envelope recreation and exciting cultural and lifestyle opportunities.